Sponsorship's Holy Grail

Sponsorship's Holy Grail

✦

Six Sigma Forges the Link Between Sponsorship & Business Goals

Raymond Bednar

iUniverse, Inc.

New York Lincoln Shanghai

Sponsorship's Holy Grail
Six Sigma Forges the Link Between Sponsorship & Business Goals

iUniverse books may be ordered through booksellers or by contacting:

iUniverse
2021 Pine Lake Road, Suite 100
Lincoln, NE 68512
www.iuniverse.com
1-800-Authors (1-800-288-4677)

ISBN-13: 978-0-595-34812-1 (pbk)
ISBN-13: 978-0-595-67158-8 (cloth)
ISBN-13: 978-0-595-79541-3 (ebk)
ISBN-10: 0-595-34812-2 (pbk)
ISBN-10: 0-595-67158-6 (cloth)
ISBN-10: 0-595-79541-2 (ebk)

Printed in the United States of America

Contents

Acknowledgements

I am indebted to a number of people who in a variety of ways made this book possible and helped shape it.

Contributing Editors

Steve Madincea, PRISM Founder and Group Managing Director

Cliff Peters, PRISM Europe Chief Executive Officer

Brian Greenwood, PRISM United Kingdom Chief Executive Officer

Special recognition goes to these PRISM colleagues who, as industry experts and reviewers, all furnished helpful suggestions and constructive criticism.

I am also grateful to editor Francis Lieder who cast as results my thoughts, experiences and expertise on this subject.

To Bruce McLaughlan, PRISM North America Managing Director, who functioned as executive editor.

To my wife Sheri and children Kelli and Matthew, whose support and patience with my unending travel schedule allowed me to find the spirit to write this book.

My thanks to all.

R.B.

Foreword

Coca-Cola. Vodafone. Ford. Olympus. Shell. Telefonica. Budweiser. Xerox. A seemingly disparate and endless list. What do they have in common? All engage in sponsorship of some magnitude to augment their sales, marketing and brand activities. Globally, sponsorship spending by brands continues to outpace almost all other forms of communication.

Sponsorship can be one of the most effective marketing tools available to an organization. It connects the passion a consumer has for a team, cause, celebrity, or property with a brand in a way that no other media can. It brings consumers in direct contact with the product or service of a company and makes that connection a part of their lives. The experiences involved in many sponsorship activities are often considered the experiences of a lifetime. The brand is present during the greatest victories, most heartfelt losses, first public viewing of art masterpieces, most memorable concerts, even successful funding of causes to help defeat diseases that have affected our lives. The emotional connections made via sponsorship last longer and reach greater depths than any traditional media campaign could ever hope to attain.

Leveraging this unique marketing tool is then a key component of successful brand and business campaigns. But proper leveraging requires extra funding. The focus quickly shifts to the questions of where is the most effective place to spend this budget and what are we really getting out of the sponsorship? Consequently, many companies have taken a stab at measuring the effectiveness of their sponsorship investments. We have seen a number of these return-on-investment models, usually developed by well intentioned individuals. But there was always a piece of the puzzle missing in these equations. *Sponsorship's Holy Grail* brings together those missing pieces.

PRISM has been at the forefront of the sponsorship game for a number of years. We were into NASCAR before it was the "in sport" in America. In Europe, we are the only agency to have been actively engaged in the prestigious UEFA Champions League since its inception. Our teams around the world have created many unique sponsorship campaigns for clients with the Olympics, the NFL, the NBA, the World Cup and Formula One.

In each instance, our clients always had to prove to their management team that they were getting true value for their sponsorship investment. That's why we created our Brand Sponsorship Valuator early in 1994. Like Microsoft, we have honed and improved our model every year to suit our client's demands. Then we took a giant leap forward with our Brand Sponsorship Valuator 6.0.

Our latest model does one thing better than anything ever before brought to bear on the sponsorship industry. It precisely measures a sponsorship investment against any combination of business or brand objectives. The PRISM leadership team of sponsorship experts has well over 200 combined years of proficiency in the field. Yet before Raymond Bednar, our CEO for North and South America, brought PRISM his analytical skills, learned at Harvard Business School and honed at Fortune 500 companies including Brown-Forman and General Electric, we were still looking for the sponsorship Holy Grail—measurability.

Why do we call this the Holy Grail of sponsorship? Executive after executive of our client companies actually coined the term for us, on first hearing that PRISM can show them how to measure all aspects of their investments in sponsorship. Just as with the mythical Grail (the Cup of Christ) sought by knights, soldiers, kings and queens for millennia, these modern knights of industry believe that discovery of true measurement processes in sponsorship will bring enlightenment. For the first time, they will be able to bring the same rigor and vigilance they exercise over all other business decisions to this important marketing investment.

That's exactly what *Sponsorship's Holy Grail* will show you. By following the methodology outlined in this book, you will make great strides on the path to enlightenment—the ability to truly understand the return on your sponsorship investment.

The key to unlocking these mysteries lies in the rigorous Six Sigma methodology, originally developed to improve manufacturing processes. Applied to sponsorship, it allows us to very clearly define what is important and what is not important in the entire process based on companies' individual business goals, and help them achieve those goals in a cost-effective manner.

As we continue to bring this process to bear on behalf of additional, diverse sponsor companies, as well as on behalf of enlightened properties, our existing processes will evolve and new ones will emerge. *Sponsorship's Holy Grail* was designed to serve as one of the first tools by which we will bring discipline to the fledgling practice of true sponsorship consultancy and an industry that has vast potential and in which we all take great pride.

It is our intention to provide additional authoritative resources in the future. We hope, based on the value you find in this text, that they will be eagerly anticipated.

Steve Madincea
PRISM
Founder &
Group Managing Director

1

What a long, strange trip it's been: Sponsorship Today

PERSPECTIVE

From a paying client's perspective, there is so much "wrong" with sponsorship today that it is hard to know where to start. But this is a bit of an over-generalization in a negative way; it's really the management of sponsorship that is in need of reformation.

American-based corporations alone spend more than $12 billion annually on sponsorship marketing—the greatest percent of that on sports sponsorship.[1] Global sponsorship spending approaches $30 billion.[2] There's a good reason for this high level of investment—quite simply, sponsorship works.

Sponsorship is a terrific way to cross borders, simplify language barriers and create tremendous emotional connections with consumers. Given that potential, a rigorous business practice methodology is no less important for sponsorship as it is for any other business expenditure. Here, we'll see why.

A few highlights from the property selling side:

The Wolf in Sheep's Clothing act. Firms cleverly sell media buys under the guise of sponsorship. These are the "halftime shows sponsored by big

---

1. IEG Sponsorship Report, 2005
2. IEG Sponsorship Report, 2005

1

company" opportunities where sponsors are convinced they are buying sponsorship—when what they are buying is expensive air time.

The Price Is Right pitch. Sponsors pay untold sums of money based upon the valuation dreamed up by the property's (the term "property" here refers to any entity—teams, people, stadiums, etc.—seeking sponsorship support) sales leader. These valuations are largely based upon the fundamental property sales question, "What do you think they would pay for Event X?"

The Media Equivalency line (or it's all about ME). Sponsors are shown figures that supposedly equate to how much they would have had to pay to generate the same advertising coverage the property generated.

The "If you don't act quickly…" myth. Usually, "We Have 20 of your closet competitors willing to buy this package in an instant if you don't buy it now." Enough said, all of us in the business have heard these utterances and may even have voiced a few ourselves.

To be completely fair, it's not all the properties' fault. Many of the wrongs today are committed by management from inside the sponsor company all by themselves! Here are a few of their highlights:

The "Wow" decision. Sometime during a business dinner, the executive responsible for sponsorship says something like, "Wow, can you imagine if we sponsored the Vatican Open? We could be playing with the Pope (or Tiger Woods, or…).

The "I Relate" decision. This one goes like this, "I relate to (golf)—more than any other thing on earth—we should sponsor (golf)."

The "Budget Round-Out" decision (increasingly losing favor today). When approached by a property to sponsor Event X for $X, the internal debate centers on, "Well, we still have $X we haven't committed this year—and this property would be "Wow" or "Related."

The "History" factor. The company has been the title sponsor FOR-EVER on this property. If you left, your dearest competitor (see "We Have 20 of your closest competitors willing to buy this package in an instant if you don't buy it now" pitch) surely will grab it.

The Inverse Fit lie. Whatever property X offers, it will find a way to fit into a needed program—often associated with "Wow" and "Related." A typical comment, "Well, it does offer a lot of entertainment opportunities with that suite they are including in the price—and we ALWAYS need to entertain, anyway."

Then there are the intrinsic, hard-wired problems with sponsorship that are not necessarily the fault of the property or the sponsor. These fall under the heading of "Turning the Queen Mary Around." They include:

Tradition. Sponsorship ALWAYS has been measured using traditional cost per thousand, Share of Voice and other typical advertising measurements. This is generally because, like advertising Return on Investment, an agency has little interest in helping a client to truly ascertain the value of the latest commercial. What if the sponsor asked the agency to share in the risk/return? Next might come sliding fees—oh no! What is wrong with this thinking is the "lag effect" inherent in sponsorship—that long time between taking the test and getting the final grade. I should add that the leading advertising agencies at WPP and elsewhere are changing this mindset to determine ROI—a quantum leap in philosophy.

The "You Cannot Value Client Entertainment" line. So much of what we define as sponsorship today is tied to entertainment that most minds are closed to the many other possibilities on which this unique and intense consumer relationship can deliver. It's always been about client entertainment, and it always will be, to their way of thinking. Again, we clearly see the role of management as it struggles to determine which weighs more: an ounce of habit or a pound of intellect.

SPONSORSHIP DEFINED

Each of the above "wrongs" will be addressed in this book. But first, let's start with a definition of exactly what is meant by the term, "sponsorship."

Definition. There is large-scale confusion as to what sponsorship means today. There are two distinctly different uses for the term "sponsorship" in common use—although they are as different as oil and water.

Media Sponsorship. Media sponsorship can consist of brand and name associations achieved with broadcast, print and internet advertising. Example: "The Half Time Show brought to you by Big Company." These have little connection with the living, breathing person watching the program. They must be coupled with additional expensive advertising time to deliver a message (or hopefully call to action) to the viewer. Think about the unaided recall of a company like Coca-Cola. Go anywhere in the world and say Coca-Cola and people know what you mean. What possible reason would Coke have to associate its famous, iconic brand name with a football half time show? Yet this is common. In this case, though, Coke is paying for media broadcast time—not sponsorship as we will define it. The relevant questions are how much they are paying for this type of media buy vs. other competitive buys in broadcast or print, and does this medium allow them to deliver a meaningful brand message?

Take-a-Note: One of the Seven Deadly Sins…

Exactly where it falls in the hierarchy is elusive, but greed has taken over an otherwise generous intention relative to sponsorship. Neither side (sponsor nor property) is without guilt in this equation. Nor are the deal-compensated agencies that are putting together the relationships. Here is the "chain of greed" in sports, as an example:

- *Owners want to win*

- *To win, owners need talented players*

- *Talented players know they only have so many years to make a career's worth of income*

- *By the way, talented players think owners are making way too much money on their backs*
- *Talented players hire agents to negotiate for a "fair deal"*
- *The "fair deal" places large financial burdens on operations*
- *Sports operations must recoup the large financial burden*
- *Sports operations raise prices on television rights, tickets, etc.*
- *Television broadcasters must charge advertisers more to pay for rights*
- *Advertisers try to charge more for their products—or cut costs of production—to cover the cost of advertising*
- *Consumers buy a more expensive product—or a product with a greater portion of its selling price going to advertising (and less of the selling price going to profit)*
- *Owner perceives people still willing to spend and…the beat goes on.*

All right, so this is a bit of a stretch. But it makes the point that greed drives greed. It's like a pack of dogs around a single bowl of dog food. "Look out for #1." "Make it while you can." "Raise the prices until people go away." You get the idea.

Greed finally comes to rest where the only real money in sponsorship resides—the sponsors. Television rates have skyrocketed, salaries have skyrocketed, stadium costs have skyrocketed. There is no economical way to pay for these massive increases simply through increased ticket prices.

But sponsors are just as greedy. They want the prime advertising slots with the prime teams—and are willing to pay for them in open competition. The properties and broadcasters froth at the mouth: "They are fighting over us!" is the cry. "Let's raise prices higher!"

Active Sponsorship. Activity-based sponsorships are the soul of this book. This is where a company (sponsor) can get into the lives of its customers. Here, we connect passion for some sort of property/person/foundation, etc., with the rational decision of whether to purchase company's products and/or services. This is the equivalent of getting on the grungy city bus, where you can see, hear and feel consumer sentiment, rather than taking a limo with sound insulation and dark glass. In active sponsorship, you (metaphorically) sit right next to the real customer and have to deliver a message that will make them love your product or service. You can't just hope like heck consumers think your new wireless service, your new vehicle, your new sandwich, is a big hit. You have to go out there and say, "Ms. Consumer, I know you love baseball—and our company does, too—how can I make you buy our product because of this connection?" This is where you win their hearts and minds—but only if you know what it is you are trying to achieve. Thus, the best-intentioned activation program will most likely fail miserably if it is not designed to be activated against company objectives.

SPONSORSHIP BENEFITS

Properly managed, sponsorship is best used for connecting a brand (product or service) to the passion of the people involved in an endeavor. The critical word here is "passion."

A person (or group of people) can be passionate about many things. We normally equate sponsorship to sports, but consumers are equally passionate about the arts, entertainment and causes. Advertising is what the brand says. Sponsorship is what the brand does. Sponsorship not only lets a brand demonstrate to consumers that its marketers like the same things they do—*it communicates that the brand likes its consumers enough to sponsor things that they care about.*

Sponsorship is just one of many marketing tools available to the marketer in order to promote and sell a product or service. It has a unique application in its ability to bring the product/service in contact with that point of passion.

By sponsoring a property (team, tour, athlete, cause, building, exhibit, etc.), the brand is trying to connect directly to the passion of the participant or the connected person/group. The goal is to connect with the passion and drive the desired behavior. This desired behavior could be loyalty, purchase intent, retention, engagement, etc.

But without passion for the sponsored property, the consumer participant may not consider the product or service. To increase the connection percentage, we try to expand the touch points. This is not limited to consumers or business-to-consumer. The same is true for business-to-business.

Here is the basic, age-old assumption: If we connect our product/service (tires, watches, consulting, etc.) to the property passion (soccer, an art exhibit, a famous band, etc), the people who are passionate about that property will be more likely to want to purchase the product or service. This traditional view of sponsorship has advantages and challenges.

Advantages. The brand is connecting the product or service to the property for all the right reasons. That connection can drive the desired behavior of the target group.

Challenges. The biggest challenge is that most companies stop right here. This is one of the reasons why name association has become so prevalent. The brand inks a deal to put field signs at the football stadium and thinks the job has been accomplished. In essence, this is expensive sign advertising—often considerably more expensive than outdoor ads along a roadside.

Our sponsorship vision extends well beyond this traditional view. There are so many more things that it can offer—almost all connecting the passion of the participant to the brand.

Bottom line. Sponsorship is a unique marketing tool that connects the brand with the emotions (passion) of a property participant. It can make a visceral connection to a consumer that traditional broadcast, print and outdoor media cannot match. To be effectively used, sponsorship demands a comprehensive marketing program that addresses a company's goals far beyond the traditional tactics of signage and brand association.

SPONSORSHIP SUCCESS FACTORS

Connecting Sponsorship to Business Goals. Later we'll see that any successful sponsorship DEMANDS a thorough understanding of ALL business goals. At this stage, we are not concerned about the goals for a particular sponsorship of any kind. Neither are we myopically concerned with just marketing goals, for example. We first must understand what makes up a successful sponsorship process for achieving the maximum number of business goals. By the way, no single sponsorship can hope to satisfy 100 percent of ideal sponsorship goals. We'll come back to this in Chapter 3.

Role of Brand Values & Attributes. Sponsorship offers the ability to connect with consumers through their passions and interests. In terms of benefiting the brand, sponsorship can enhance brand values. Through association with something about which the consumer is passionate, the migration of brand values can create, reinforce or change brand perceptions. It also can increase brand relevance. Sponsorship can be effective in making a brand relevant to the lives and interests of consumers and creating memorable moments with them in places where they have chosen to be.

Increasing brand credibility is another function. The brand value migration that takes place in sponsorship, not only with the event itself but also with the brand's positioning alongside fellow co-sponsors, can increase credibility. Sponsorship can communicate product benefits. By providing independent endorsement for claims made in advertising, sponsorship can help to communicate product benefits. A brand also can benefit from the perception that it has been chosen for partnership by the event—this can portray the brand as a leader in its field, if the property is well-respected. Finally, provided the event or activity is not cluttered with too many other co-sponsors, the right sponsorship can build brand awareness. Fully integrated into other channels, sponsorship undertaken for this reason can be successful at building awareness outside of traditional channels.

The Importance of Activation. Activation brings a sponsorship to life. An example would be that of a wrist watch product line seeking to be the official timepiece of the Super Bowl. What does a watch have to do with the Super Bowl? Well, assume that the goal is to get access to the same audience that the product serves. This can be a good strategy—if it is activated in the manner described in this book. However, this sometimes takes the form of "Naming Rights"—stadiums, arenas, events, etc. The thinking behind the assumption goes like this: If we put our name all over a property then people who admire/like that property will want to buy our product or service. An interesting philosophical approach—but this is NOT true activation which occurs through select communication channels.

HOW SPONSORSHIP IS USED

So how do most companies use sponsorship today? Here are a few examples.

Endorsement. A famous person endorses the product, then people who admire/like that person will want to buy the product or service. A risky approach at best, this could end up with the endorser disgraced in some way.

As a brand association. "Our brand is not strong enough on its own two spindly little legs so let's associate it with another stronger brand or property." Often this produces poorly constructed or disconnected associations that confuse target customers.

As a form of advertising. Most often, this has to do with brand positioning and brand association. Both are plausible, real uses of marketing dollars—sponsors just have to understand that what they are engaging in is really advertising, not sponsorship. By the same token, advertising is no substitute for other essential business communication activities such as good public relations, especially where new brands are concerned: new brands need the credibility only publicity can provide.

To accomplish business objectives. This does actually occur, albeit in an interesting derivative to what I will suggest. In most sponsorships today, the client company tries to "fit" the sponsorship into whatever objectives it thinks can be achieved with the property. Too often, though, these objectives are disconnected from the real business objectives. Further, this lack of connection to business objectives is neither comprehensive nor subject to the same rigorous ROI scrutiny as other investments.

COMMON "BUSINESS OBJECIVES"

Many so-called business objectives cited as justification for companies' sponsorship programs wouldn't have credibility if they were applied to any other field. Here are some of the most frequently cited objectives companies hope to achieve with their sponsorship activities:

Client entertainment. This is a part of nearly all sponsorship programs. This is not to say that client entertainment is not a business objective; on the contrary, it is almost always a business objective. I firmly believe it is an essential part of all business. The old saw about "…got more business done during a five-hour golf outing than years of office meetings," is true. The question is not whether a company should have client entertainment as part of its sponsorship program. The real question is why a company would use the costly and complicated route of sponsorship for this goal when it could just as easily buy the best tickets to whatever sporting event is the most important to the client. For most companies, negotiations are focused (if they negotiate anything) on number of tickets, location of suite, use of trademarks, production days, etc. Most negotiations start from a position of weakness: the property high-balls the opening figure and the company responds by negotiating a satisfactory price…instead of negotiating based on value. In any case, the response is necessarily a reaction to an offer from the property—it is not biased from the start (as it should be) with the sponsors' goals in mind.

Sales incentive. This normally manifests itself in a sales program aimed at the distribution channel. Example: Top 10 sales people go to the Master's Golf Tournament.

Consumer incentive. Often on-packaging, free-standing package inserts or collateral campaigns aimed at driving desired consumer behavior. Example: Buy so many bottles of soft drinks, fill out the attached form, send it in with bottle caps, and get to go to the Big Name Soft Drink Company Event.

Employee reward/morale. Often tied to employee retention, performance management, attendance, length of service, etc. Example: Season tickets to a professional sports team's home games after 10 years of service.

SEGMENTS OF SPONSORSHIP

If we assume this is how sponsorship is used today, these are the common segments of investment:

Sports. Often, "sponsorship" is considered synonymous with sports. Sponsorship involves many other segments of the potential market. Sports are just one of the higher-profile vehicles that have been used for the past century. Sub-segments within the sports genre include: celebrities, teams, naming rights, events, etc. I believe the sports category is the most significant area of sponsorship abuse today, for the following reasons.

First, overall, valuations are absurd. Valuations have completely separated from reality. There are few, if any, real connections between sponsorship fees and the value they provide to the sponsor.

Second, comparative valuations are the second reason. If the NASCAR market is commanding a $10-million price tag for a single driver, then $10 million to place company branding on every shirt of an entire soccer team must be a bargain, right?

Third, sports entities are dictating the terms of sponsorship engagement. The sports franchise usually initiates the bidding process on sponsorship and remains in control throughout the negotiations. The reasons are two-fold. First, sponsors generally have little idea of what they are trying to achieve with their sponsorship programs, so they accept what is offered. What is offered is a package that represents the least possible work for the property. Second, owners know the going prices within their sport, their particular segment and their team. They KNOW approximately what everyone else is paying to be in the game. Although no one openly dis-cusses these numbers, they are transmitted between the connected parties just like any other business.

Another reason is the hubris involved. If, to use a metaphor, egos play a huge part in all sponsorship, then the sports segment is Muhammad Ali. There is much at stake within the inner circles as to feelings of adequacy and superiority of a player, team or franchise. Winning is the foundation of sports and sponsorship fees are just another mark on the scorecard. These intense emotions help drive this segment to the far edges of restraint in fee negotiations.

Last, the demand for iconic player participation raises basic entry level fees. Recently, former marathon world record holder Khalid Khannouchi agreed to a four-year deal with the Chicago Marathon, guaranteeing the race will be his only fall marathon through 2007 (USA Today, Thursday, May 20, 2004, Page 13c, Update column). Someone has to pay for this guaranteed participation and that someone has to be the media or the sponsors, which are just other forms of revenue sources to the property.

Entertainment. A close cousin to sports is entertainment. Sports are entertainment, of course. However, for the purposes of this book we are characterizing this category by including properties such as concerts, tours, plays, movies, etc. This category often is overlooked or overshadowed by sports.

Arts. Defined as museum shows, exhibits, theatrical works and normally classical musical series. Arts can be the most efficient and effective way to reach specific high-income level targets and corporate management suites. This category has been a tough one to grow from a property standpoint because these activities rarely provide any type of large scale utilization in the way that sports do. In addition, this highly efficient category is underutilized due to the lack of measurement sophistication by most arts organizations.

Not-for-profits. Defined to include certain altruistic for-profits, as well. These include special interests, disease associations, foundations, etc. These are supported mainly through foundation (shareholder) funds in large companies. They don't seem to come under the return on investment (ROI) microscope as much as other segments. I believe this to be the case because the ROI is emotionally or intrinsically inferred by the nature of the property itself.

Major conventions and business gatherings. Often relegated to "events" management, and rarely being a centralized marketing function, this segment is sadly under-utilized and subject to the same pigeon-holing sports sponsorship faces. The most common application is the dreaded trade show, where a company displays the obligatory booth and staff fields questions that rarely generate business from passers-by who have no buying power anyway. This is a great vehicle for a slicer-dicer TV product but very ineffective for a corporation trying to achieve real multi-business function goals. Ideally, "shows" should be a voice to a company's current and prospective customers. They should be used to demonstrate dominance in product or knowledge. Trade shows are often highlighted by the presentations of major speakers. Although traditionally thought of as a passive activity, trade shows can communicate aggressively with proper management.

SPONSORSHIP LEVELS

Within the above categories, often there are differing "levels" of sponsorship. These levels include:

Sole or Title Sponsor. Clearly "owning the title" as the only sponsor or as the creator of an event to meet a need.

Official Sponsor. One of a small number of equal sponsors with the same rights and status.

Official Supplier. Providers of technical or other support to the event but possessing a sponsorship with far less value or clout.

All are "descriptive" terms used to associate a sponsor's status with a property. This labeling often is used to drive values. "Naming sponsor" versus "official partner" normally have significantly differing values associated with their placards. Naming rights, brand association and many other considerations are involved. This hierarchy of rights allows a property to stratify its selling structure. Another way to look at it is an airline selling a coach class seat next to a business class seat on the same flight. The flight does end at the same destination. With tiered sponsorship, however, the end result is what was negotiated (or left to chance) in terms of reaching business goals.

THE BIG DISCONNECT

So how did such a well-intentioned idea of providing a local sports team with a little extra cash in return for them putting your brand on the stadium go so wrong? Here are a few of the contributing disconnects driving the Big Disconnect:

Using sponsorship to sell cars. This goal is ineffective as a tool because there's too much "noise" between the sponsored event and the consumer's decision to purchase a car…unless the cars are sold at the sponsorship event itself. One could locate vehicles at a highly visible stadium venue (the kind of access that only an expensive sponsorship could provide), sell the cars on the spot, including turn-key financing, licensing and all other requirements, and let the new owner drive the car away. In this case, sponsorship would have been directly connected to selling cars. In any other approach, what statisticians call "noise in the process" overwhelms the cause-effect relationship. What is noise? Noise is any sort of variable action/elements that affect the desired outcome of a process.

Since at-stadium sales might be cumbersome, instead of selling cars right at the sponsored property, the brand mark is exhibited via signage or displays and its supposed impact on sales is monitored at the surrounding dealerships. Good in theory, but this approach still reflects massive noise in the process. Here, noise could include the unaccountable effect of the amount and timing of rebates, incentives, media advertising, discounts, word of mouth, competitive product availability or attractiveness, etc. It's like pushing a boat with a rope; there's no direct connection between realizable objectives and reality.

Thus, it appears that the sponsorship's ability to help reach the business goal of selling cars cannot be DIRECTLY measured in terms of a return on investment (ROI). This conclusion would be correct if not for the disciplined Six Sigma approach used in this book.

Media sponsorships drive values. In reality, media sponsorships simply are broadcast rights. In many cases, this is expensive advertising. An advertising agency should be used to help make these important media buying decisions.

"Opportunities" vs. Business Goals. Normally well-grounded, rational business people can be lured into "opportunities." Opportunities can drive the decision-making process. Business goals are then fit to the opportunities. In effect, these are distractions with perks negotiated for unneeded things.

The Lag Time Problem. Brand image/association takes too long to measure. It' only becomes evident after the fact if it was a good or bad idea. It's like looking in a rear-view mirror to judge the value (however incalculable) much after the effect—and the money, at this point, is gone.

TAKE-AWAY

And that's the way it is, helping to make sponsorship what it is today:

An odd and unreasonable mix of activation efforts, management confusion and rising prices, with advertising expenses helping to drive the cost equation.

But there is a means of subjecting sponsorship to a rational process that seeks to measure its performance against real business goals. This method is based on the principles of the management tool known as Six Sigma, which is introduced in the next chapter.

2

A Sponsorship Vision for the Future

In Chapter One, we saw how sponsorship is frequently misused, misunderstood or misvalued, even by companies with very comprehensive "sponsorship programs."

Have faith, all is not doom and gloom for sponsorship. A rational management approach that takes into account strategic positioning and fact-based decision making can turn a program into a dynamic contributor to the marketing mix.

A STUDY IN VALUE CREATION

Let's start with a vision of "enlightened leadership." By the way, the funny-looking "o" next to the 6 is the Greek symbol for "sigma."

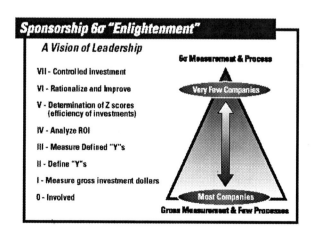

Handwritten annotations at top: "Involved → Spend" "Enlightenment" "5" "Act. Spending ≤ 100% of Sponsorship"

Level 0—Basic Involvement. Along the left side of this chart is an ascending hierarchy of Zen-like vision attainment. At the bottom, "0", is where the vast majority of companies dwell that use sponsorship, regardless of how much they are spending. These are the companies buying sponsorship to fulfill some perceived need. A common reason to enter sponsorship is to counter the competition. A simple litmus test for determining if a company is at this level is a quick analysis of the ratio of activation to sponsorship spending.

As an example, let's assume a company is paying $2 million for the naming rights at a professional sports stadium. At the same time, it is spending untracked token amounts on client entertainment (activation) in addition to the naming rights expenditure. If this ratio of activation spending to sponsorship spending is below five percent, we could say this company's enlightenment is characterized as "Level 0—Involved." In this example, this would mean that entertainment spending is approximately $100,000. This seems like a lot of spending for just being "involved," not to mention the fact that it might be misspent money.

Now think about what can be realistically done with $100,000. A relatively minor golf outing connected to a major tour sponsorship will often carry a budget of more than $50,000 (including rooms, flights, meals, green fees, etc.). Nearly the same objective can be achieved independently without spending the original $2 million for the naming rights simply by staging a world-class golf outing. The example highlights a hypothetical (and all too real) sponsor who is not connecting the sponsorship (and consumer passion) to business goals. Client entertainment may be a goal but why is sponsorship needed to achieve it?

Level I—Measurement of Gross Investment Dollars. Just above "Involved" is the next level of measuring *exactly* what is spent on the sponsorship. The operative word is "exactly."

Nearly all sponsors know what they pay for the right to sponsor. This may include incremental costs such as buying additional tickets, hotel rooms, etc. Few, if any, track exactly what is being invested in the relationship because few understand why they are in the relationship. For the time being, let's leave this level with an understanding that someone at Level I is tracking "gross"—not exact—investment in the property/activity.

Level II—Definition of "Y"s. "Y"s are goals for a process as defined by Six Sigma. Many sponsorship managers think they are defining "goals" for their company's participation in a property by listing broad and mostly vague marketing and sales objectives, such as:

- Entertaining clients
- Associating the brand with the property
- Getting more business

Since these do not reflect the underlying elements of the objectives, these are not Y's in the context of our process. Short examples: at minimum, "getting more business" could be broken into the underlying elements of "fewer cancellations" or "selling additional services." Entertaining clients could be broken into reaching "decision makers" or "salespeople."

To characterize the entire equation: Getting more business (Y) is a function (f) of x (the underlying elements). Or $Y = f(x)$.

Level III—Measuring Defined Y's. Now that the Y Definition stage has been achieved, interaction with the property to be measured can be designed from the very start. Most sponsorship and client measurement systems are designed to provide data that they already collect. Briefly, these two data collection systems consist of processes that are designed to provide information that is easily collected for the property. This data includes attendance, media coverage, reach, etc. Additionally, these measurement systems are most often oriented to long-term data collection. They data include Share of Voice, periodic sales reports, ongoing general market research, etc.

Both systems are of only general interest to the new sponsorship measurement method advocated here. The Y Discernment process helps the sponsoring company determine the supporting elements of a particular Y. This is discussed in detail later. For now, it will suffice to say that the enlightened model emphasizes the imperative of designing the sponsorship to be measured against the goals for entering into the relationship. The existing data set may or may not be relevant to the new Y's.

Level IV—Analysis of ROI. Now that we know the critical Y's can be defined and used to measure the success of the sponsorship relationship, we can develop a Return on Investment (ROI). ROI is simple in theory, but usually more difficult to determine in practice. This disjunction is due to the misalignment of company goals with sponsorship attributes from the outset.

The aim is to design measurement of the sponsorship property to be conducted from the start. This allows anticipation of ROI models that are built and tested in advance against predetermined hurdles.

The objective in measuring ROI is to determine what portion of an investment is returned in the form of measurable results.

Level V—Determination of Z Scores (**efficiency of investments**). As the hierarchy is ascended, the "efficiency" of any investment can be determined. Efficiency is a metric used to determine how well scarce resources are producing results. Let's take an example: Think of the fuel efficiency of cars. One car gets 30 miles per gallon, the other 15 miles per gallon. This doesn't mean the car with 30 miles per gallon is a better car than the 15 miles per gallon car at all. It simply means in the ONE task—efficiency of fuel consumption—the 30 mile per gallon car rates higher. That 30 mile per gallon vehicle may also accommodate only two people—making it entirely impractical for moving a large group.

In our determination of efficiencies of sponsorship investments we are trying to accomplish the same thing. Namely, to know which sponsorship opportunity will produce best on the same amount of resources? There may well be compelling reasons that can overshadow this metric—as in the two-person car being impractical for a large group. Independent of any of these other reasons though, we essentially are trying to determine which sponsorship investment is the most efficient in delivering on the goals we have designed our measurement of the investment to demonstrate.

Beyond this initial value, our application of this theory is "dimensionless." What does this mean? Unlike the 30 mpg example above, our sponsorship efficiency model is not "qualified"—it is not restricted in its use and comparative function to one metric, such as fuel efficiency. Miles per gallon cannot be used to compare which car is faster, which hauls more, etc. The dimensionless efficiency model, however, allows us to compare different activities which are trying to achieve widely different objectives.

An example is summarized in the chart below:

Segment	Property	Y	Goal	Z
Sports	PGA	Employee Retention	85% Participation	1.5
Art	Monet Exhibit	Name Capture	$5 Per Name	2.0
Entertainment	Rolling Stones Tour	Product Demo	500 Trials Per Concert	3.0

Notice we are comparing three different sponsorship segments—sports, arts and entertainment. In each segment, we are using a different property to achieve a different goal. For example, in the Art segment we are using a Monet art exhibit for the purpose of capturing names of potential customers with the goal being a cost of $5 per name (after we pay for the sponsorship and all the activities associated with capturing those names). That activity has an efficiency of "2.0" and compares to the other two examples favorably and unfavorably. So which is better, a smaller efficiency number or a larger? It's the same as fuel efficiency—the larger the number, the more efficient the process is at achieving the goal for which it has been designed. The 3.0 score of Entertainment is the most efficient in this comparison. The calculation of a Z Score will be discussed in detail later in this book.

Higher Z → more efficient

Level V is a critical level because it denotes the ability to determine which investment among competing offers requiring scarce resources is the most efficient.

Level VI—Rationalize, Improve and DOE. Advancing still further up the hierarchy, now that we can know how efficient the various sponsorships are, we can determine which to keep, which to dispose of and which to improve. Here we realize the true cost savings in the Six Sigma process. Let's review Rationalization, Improvement and DOE separately.

A. Rationalization. Referring back to the chart used above, we may elect to eliminate the PGA event because of its low Z score relative to the alternatives. On the other hand, we may choose to use it to achieve another goal for which it may offer a more efficient relationship.

Decisions on rationalizing the sponsorship investment are based upon many factors in addition to ROI and Z scores. Common discriminators include overall cost limits, long-term property commitment, management affinity, segment coverage requirements, goal coverage, and the use of financial tools such as net present value, internal rate of return, and payback period.

As each company will have its own set of evaluation criteria, it is not possible to outline a "boilerplate" set of guidelines to analyze such a complex management decision. However, I recommend that any set of criteria contain an exercise in which five important sponsorship questions are used to interrogate any current or prospective sponsorship opportunity. Briefly, the questions are:

1. What business goal(s) does the sponsorship seek to affect?
2. What business goal(s) could the sponsorship affect?
3. How do you know the goal is being affected—how do you know you are being successful?
4. How do you measure the long term performance of achieving the goal?

5. How do you measure the short term (in-process) achievement of the goal?

Further, the Six Sigma process gives a company the ability to clearly understand the business implications of yield on sponsorship investments. What they choose to do with this knowledge remains the privilege of the corporate suite.

Rationalization of this type will provide the company with a very powerful set of analytical tools to reduce waste and increase the return on investment. This result alone often pays for the investment in the Six Sigma management process.

B. Improvement. Improving the return on a company's investment in sponsorships that survive the rationalization process is the second huge gain from adopting a Six Sigma based sponsorship management program. This step is combined with rationalization because the two are inextricably linked in the management decision process. The rationalization process often is linked to the perceived ability to improve the performance of the potential surviving sponsorship candidates. Conversely, the perceived ability to improve the performance of a relationship may be a key determinant in the rationalization process.

So let's discuss the improvement process that will be applied to the survivors. Improvement in both the ROI and Z score of a particular investment normally is obtained using many simple management tools. Examples include eliminating unfocused ancillary programs and increasing spending on existing programs or program elements. For example, if the "Coffee with the NASCAR Pit Crew Chief" is consistently providing quality consumer data, it may warrant expansion. If not, it should be re-evaluated and either improved or eliminated, and the money invested elsewhere.

C. Design of Experiments. In the Six Sigma process, there is a methodology called, "design of experiments," or DOEs. DOEs are simply the application of rudimentary scientific inquiry. Let's focus on the word "experiment."

To experiment is to hold certain elements of a program constant while varying other elements in order to determine the effect of the variation on the overall outcome of the process. Let's take a simple, real-life example.

The process of obtaining data on an individual consumer is a common goal of many direct interaction programs associated with sponsorship. All one has to do is attend a sporting event to find a credit card issuer with a table offering gifts in exchange for the consumer opting to give certain personal information such as name, address, income, etc. The possibilities for experimenting with the yield of such an operation are numerous. One could:

Set up the sign-up tables in totally opposite sites within the stadium to determine if location has any effect on yield of obtaining information—is the location near the food stands better than the location near the entrance, or near the bathrooms?

Set up the tables with different and mutually exclusive gift offerings—perhaps a tote bag at one and a stuffed animal at another—what gifts are more conducive to improving yield?

Set up the tables outside the stadium—perhaps near the cars to see if yield improves or declines—signaling a potential savings in cost by identifying easier location set-up (and perhaps lower site or set up fees). The variations are endless.

The point is that certain portions of the experiment are held constant—the same stadium, the same game, the same credit card, etc., while changing other portions to determine if the performance of the activity can be improved.

This process is systematically used to improve the outcome of an investment.

Level VII—Controlled Investments. The apex of the hierarchy. Once we have rationalized and improved investments we must maintain the new level of return by setting limits on the processes used to reach these results.

Controlling process means setting up reporting limits to signal when investments are going "out of control." Out of control means a process is yielding results that are not within the expected range of results.

To understand when a process is either "in" or "out" of control, we need reporting tools that gather and organize data in an easily understandable format. This is normally a process of management by exception rather than active analysis. In other words, we don't necessarily need to know that the process is in control—we expect that because we have invested in building a process to achieve the new performance level. Instead, we want to know when the process has crossed the boundaries of acceptable control levels.

A sample control chart is illustrated here:

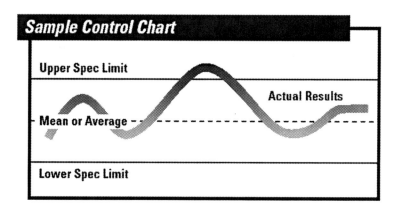

Here you see the line varies along the middle of the chart—or the mean. The line above the center line is the upper control limit and the bottom line is the lower control limit. As long as the results—the varying line in the middle—stay within the upper and lower limits, the process is "in control." When the line crosses the upper or lower limits, it is not in control.

This information is critical to the management process so that we are clearly alerted to take action to bring the process back into control and maintain the hard-fought gains when necessary.

In order to report more completely on a group of activities, we may use a slightly more sophisticated format than the graph above. PRISM's report format is the "dashboard." The name refers to its graphic similarity of how a car dashboard looks and works. Dashboards give a driver various data on how the car is performing. Examples include speed, tachometer, oil pressure, coolant temperature, fuel level, etc. The same theory is used in designing "dashboard" reports for sponsorship. Chapter 8 discusses dashboards in more depth.

TAKE-AWAY

Crafting a visionary program for sponsorship as part of a company's marketing mix is not only possible, it is imperative. Pressure from investors and increasing needs for evidence of return on investment demand a rigorous program of thoughtful and structured sponsorship strategy. Gone are the days of whimsical investments into golf, tennis and the like. A logical, comprehensive system to develop an investment mindset about sponsorship is a requirement. Fortunately, it's also a reality.

3

The Six Sigma Connection

Enter the need for a way to systematically bring sponsorship under objective scrutiny. All other forms of business and marketing investments have faced this kind of analytical rigor for decades.

Don't be frightened into thinking you'll now have to learn how Six Sigma is going to solve all the problems and challenges identified above. We're simply going to use this extremely well-proven methodology to provide a framework for thoughtful consideration in using sponsorship as part of the overall marketing mix.

So don't quit reading because you think, "Here comes the rocket science." This is a book on how PRISM has used Six Sigma to develop a process that brings discipline, order and thoughtful decision-making to the Wild, Wild, West of sponsorship. Rest assured, you can understand it. Let's start with the basics.

WHAT IS SIX SIGMA?

In its most basic definition, Six Sigma is a mathematical/statistical-based process that seeks to measure the performance of a process or a product. It was developed at Motorola in the mid-1980s as a way to detect manufacturing defects per million opportunities. Up until that time, the standard measurement was defects per thousand opportunities. Increases in production efficiencies, coupled with the demands for ever-higher quality products, forced this transition.

Take-a-Note: The Origin of Six Sigma

"...our quality stinks!"

—*Motorola executive Art Sundry*

Back in 1979, when most American companies believed that quality cost money, Motorola realized that done right, improving quality would actually reduce costs. At the time, the company was spending as much as 20 percent, or $800 million to $900 million annually, correcting poor quality—the "inspiration" for Mr. Sundry's comment.

Meanwhile, one of their engineers, Bill Smith, had been quietly studying the correlation between the field life of a product and how often that product had been repaired during the manufacturing process. He presented findings that concluded that if a product was found defective and corrected during manufacturing, other defects were bound to be missed and discovered during early use by the customer.

He also concluded, however, that when the product was manufactured error-free, it rarely failed during early use. His work was greeted with skepticism until the company began finding out that foreign competitors were making error-free products during manufacturing. Motorola began its quest to improve quality, and simultaneously improve production time and costs, by focusing on how the product was designed and made.

It was this link between higher quality and lower cost that led to the development of Six Sigma—an initiative that at first focused on improving quality through the use of exact measurements to anticipate problem areas, not just react to them. In other words, Six Sigma would allow business leaders to be proactive rather than reactive.

Proof of its value materialized when Motorola applied Six Sigma to its Bandit pager, which hit the marketplace with a life-expectancy of 150 years and was so reliable, it was cheaper to replace it than to again test the virtually error-free product. Within four years, Six Sigma had saved the company $2.2 billion. From there, Six Sigma spread like wildfire to other industries—and beyond manufacturing divisions alone.—Excerpted from Pande & Holpe, What is Six Sigma? Doubleday 2000.

Six Sigma is a total management commitment and philosophy of excellence, customer focus, process improvement and the application of measurement rather than gut feel. Sponsorship Six Sigma is about making any area of the organization better able to meet the changing needs of customers and markets. How?

Focus on the Customer. Marketers have long known the importance of really understanding consumers. In Six Sigma, customer focus becomes THE top priority. Six Sigma improvements begin with the customer and are defined by their impact on customer satisfaction and value.

Data- & Fact-Driven Management. Amazingly, most sponsorship business decisions are still based on opinions and assumptions. Six Sigma helps sponsorship managers answer two essential questions to support data-driven decisions and solutions. What data do I really need? How do I use it to maximum benefit?

Processes Are Where The Action Is. Six Sigma positions THE PROCESS as the key vehicle of success. One of the most remarkable breakthroughs to date—particularly in service-based industries and functions—is that mastering processes builds competitive advantage in delivering value. And processes can be REPLICATED. Does anyone really know how to replicate gut feel?

Proactive Management. Proactive management means making habits out of business practices: defining goals; reviewing them frequently; setting clear priorities; focusing on problem prevention; and QUESTIONING why we do things instead of blindly defending them.

Boundaryless Collaboration. Boundarylessness is simply working to improve teamwork up, down and across organizational lines. Billions of dollars are lost every day because of competition between groups that should be working toward a common cause.

Emphasis on New Ideas & Approaches. Introducing new ideas is not without risk. But people who see possible ways to be closer to perfect are not afraid of the consequences of mistakes—if they were, they'd never try in the first place. By the same token, there's no "one right way." Organizations are different and the differences justify varying approaches to Six Sigma.

So what's Six Sigma's goal? A process that is operating within Six Sigma parameters will only have 3.4 defects per million opportunities. Put into context, if a manufacturing process involves connecting two pieces of sheet metal with a single metal screw, that operation will only be "defective" 3.4 times in one million operations!

So how does this type of manufacturing process control apply to a discipline like marketing and sponsorship? Better yet, why would you apply this discipline to marketing and sponsorship? The answer lies below—in the core of Six Sigma.

THE CORE OF SIX SIGMA

The core process used in nearly all applications of Six Sigma centers around five stages identified by a simple acronym: DMAIC. DMAIC stands for:

Define
Measure
Analyze
Improve
Control

1. Define. If we want to measure our ability to achieve any goal (thus greatly enhancing the replicability of such results), we first have to identify the goal we are trying to achieve. This is the essence of the Define stage. We need to clearly define what the desired outcome of the process should be. In manufacturing this may be a statement such as:

"Mill an aluminum bar to the dimensions of 20mm in length, by 20mm in width, by 10mm in height—plus or minus 0.0001mm in any direction."

In sponsorship Six Sigma, this is a critical and often painfully difficult stage for sponsors. They are not certain what they are trying to achieve as an end result, beyond the traditional belief that sponsorship is for entertaining and perhaps promotion.

2. Measure. Once we define the goal, we can begin measuring how well it is being met. This involves a process called base-lining. Base-lining is measuring how well the goal was met using the existing process prior to introducing any Six Sigma improvement techniques. This is important as it identifies if progress is being made. Beyond base-lining, Measure is a continual process of assessing progress toward the goal specified in the Define stage. Measures may include physical counts, research analytics, simple and/or complex observations, etc.

3. Analyze. The measurements normally consist of raw data. This may be a set of numbers such as total people attending an event—subcategorized by ethnicity, sex, income, education, etc. The Analyze stage converts the raw data into meaningful and relevant information gleaned from statistics and other metrics as defined by the measurer.

4. Improve. The Analyze stage provides plenty of statistics to consider in an examination of goal attainment. The gap between the measured results and the definition of the goal is then the object for improvement. In the Improve stage, we undertake experiments (often referred to as Designs of Experiments, or DOEs) to determine if holding certain program elements constant while varying other parts will lead to a greater reduction in deviation from the target value. As part of a baseball sponsorship package, we may set up a table at the stadium with the goal of collecting names for later solicitation (the typical credit card table at many sporting events). We may conduct a DOE by varying the incentive give-away product at different games. All other aspects remain the same—the table, the set up, the baseball stadium, etc. The only thing varied is the incentive. At one game we may try a cap, at another a t-shirt, and at yet another perhaps a logo watch. During the Improve stage, adjustments are made based on data.

5. Control. Now that gains in achieving the goal have been made, gains must be controlled. Six Sigma is not a process without costs. Much will be invested in achieving the gains and we need to ensure we don't slide backward. This involves the use of ongoing metrics and reporting systems that alert the sponsor to any drop in performance.

Volumes have been written on each of these stages. However, at this point, it is sufficient for the reader to understand *that our process seeks continual improvement toward goals defined in the first stage using measurement, analytics, improvement techniques and control reports.* This is a simple process that has broad applicability across many segments of business.

<u>SIX SIGMA IS RIGHT FOR MARKETING IN GENERAL</u>

Six Sigma is about process control. It is not about stifling creativity—it is about facilitating and channeling its effectiveness. If you think about it, almost all marketing functions involve processes intended to eventually influence a purchase decision. Let's explore an example of a traditional marketing process—packaging.

Most marketers of retail products consider the packaging to be an integral part of the marketing and selling function. Bringing that packaging to life on a shelf takes a process. Here are some of the elements:

Graphics design. The package usually must conform to some overall packaging guidelines that preserve and promote the larger brand identity. For example, retail products have to conform to the corporate identity guidelines.

Packaging specifications. The package must survive shipment and still look good on the shelf.

Product features and benefits. Most packaging will list the features and benefits of the product in a manner consistent with the larger brand and company messages.

Labeling. There are many labeling requirements. These may include weight, UPC codes, certificate of origin, etc. Food packaging may require the nutritional data disclosure label with which we have all become so familiar.

While this is only a brief listing of the many elements involved in a retail package, it helps to illustrate the many processes and sub-processes involved with the marketing function of packaging development and delivery.

Each of the processes has a chance for error. One simple example involves the bar code. I was involved with a new product for one of the largest retailers in the world. We checked that the bar code numbers printed directly below the actual vertical bar codes on the packaging matched with the product identification. We did not actually use a scanning device to see if the numbers matched what the bar codes represented. Needless to say, the vertical bar codes did not match the numbers—causing a large cost increase to re-mark the packages.

This is a good example of what can go wrong with a process that does not undergo Six Sigma scrutiny to ensure quality. We would have saved considerable time, energy and anxiety if we had applied rigorous quality processes to the steps in producing the bar codes. As always, we would have started with the most basic of all Six Sigma mantras—understand the process—and all the elements that constitute its successful conclusion. In this case, a strong understanding of the bar code development process would have helped avoid the costly redesign.

In terms of its relationship to sponsorship, the same basic Six Sigma mantra of understanding the process is the foundation of illuminating the world of sponsorship and points up why a company would want to use it as a marketing tool.

Sponsorship is a process. For a sponsor, it is a process that starts with a clear understanding of what needs to be achieved using sponsorship. In the sheet metal fastening example, the goal was to achieve a maximum defect per million rate of 3.4 or less. The process of joining the two pieces of sheet metal has been given a goal of only 3.4 defects per million opportunities.

The metal forming company has identified this level of quality as essential to the overall product selling success. It has set a quantifiable goal. This is the first fundamental building block of Six Sigma.

THE ESSENTIALS OF SIX SIGMA

I have said that the five steps of Six Sigma are DMAIC—**D**efine, **M**easure, **A**nalyze, **I**mprove and **C**ontrol. But those steps are founded upon the general concept of the need for goals, measurement and the importance of immediate, in-process feedback. Let's look at each of them.

Sponsorship Six Sigma Essential #1—Goals. This methodology forces thinking about goals for the use of sponsorship. Let's take a look at where most advanced/enlightened companies START and END with sponsorship goals. For instance, a global energy drinks company may have the following goals.

Sponsors' Goals

Marketing Objectives (as an example)

- Increase unaided recall 2 points
- Direct market nutrition products
- Increase Brand Awareness Men 24+
- Establish USA Hispanic base
- Create trial at 14 yr age level
- Expand into South America
- Drive service free income
- Become product of choice among professionals

Later we'll see that the start of any successful sponsorship DEMANDS a thorough understanding of ALL the business goals the sponsor would ideally address using sponsorship. We are not concerned about the goals for this particular sponsorship. Further, to avoid being pigeon-holed, we are not merely concerned with marketing goals. We seek to understand what makes up a successful sponsorship process for achieving the maximum number of business goals. In the graphic below, the hash marks represent distinct goals within in each business area:

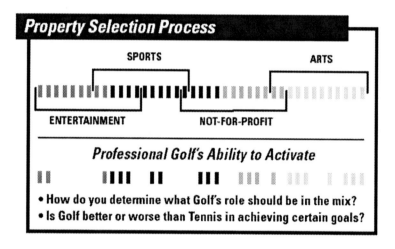

By the way, no single sponsorship can hope to satisfy 100 percent of ideal sponsorship goals.

In the ultimate application of this process, the tables will be turned on the properties and those properties that can meet the greatest portion of an ideal set of sponsorship goals will emerge. But goals alone are not enough. They must also be measurable. This is the second fundamental building block of Six Sigma—measurement of goals.

Sponsorship Six Sigma Essential #2—Measurement. This methodology forces thinking about how to quantify goals associated with the property.

Think about sponsorship in this way: How many quantifiable goals are there for each program? How well is it done? How do you know? What is the process of doing it well? Do weeks pass before you know? Do you find out when the sponsorship is in operation or only afterward? How/can you affect performance in-process?

Nearly all companies track progress in the use of sponsorship by long-term methods. Traditional metrics include market share, share of voice, Nielsen ratings, sales, etc. These metrics are critical to the success of any marketing program. The challenge in using them exclusively is that they are historical reports by their very nature. They help to explain whether or not something worked—but they don't tell us—***in process***—if the goals are going to be met.

Here is a typical spending curve for a company using a process to capture qualified names.

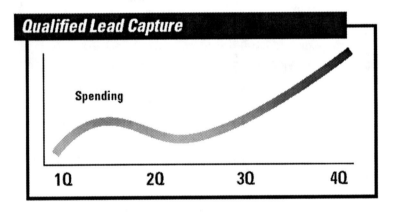

This is common for a credit card company or any company trying to gain access to what it determines to be fertile hand-raisers for its product. The x-axis is just time—first quarter, second quarter, etc. The y-axis is spending level. Notice how it starts off in the first quarter moving up and then begins leveling off as it starts into the second quarter and eventually starts declining. This is a typical reaction often associated with the inability to determine cause and effect of the spending. As the company spends money on this name-capture activity, it doesn't immediately perceive a benefit. This can lead to a wait and hold attitude as the managers try to figure out if the name-capture process is working. Once the process appears to be working (by some definition of success) the spending will start again, as depicted in the below chart.

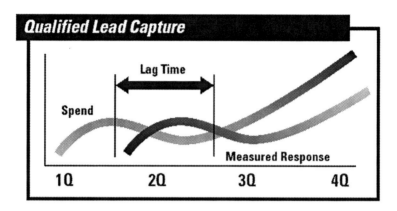

In this chart, we see the measured response kicking in—often based on advertising measures such as share of voice and unaided recall. The delay between the two critical stages is noted by the vertical lines labeled, "Lag Time." One of the problems with using these types of measures is that they are historical in nature. That is, they tell what happened—but not what *is happening* as spending occurs—at least in the short-term. The result is a large expense associated with determining if this approach to name capturing activity is working.

Perhaps because of my West Point background, I like to use a Pentagon missile analogy here. The above example is the management equivalent of firing a multi-million dollar missile at a target and missing it to the left. The correction in the firing platform is made (hopefully a little more to the right the second time) and a second missile is fired. It misses to the right so another correction is made, etc. Meanwhile, millions of dollars are being spent firing missiles and making corrections based upon where they land! I think most would agree this is a highly wasteful and inefficient way to spend. For the record, the Pentagon doesn't test missiles this way—it's just an irresistible analogy.

measure as u go / proacutive not reactive

Instead of firing the missile and seeing where it lands, we need a built-in guidance control module. That is EXACTLY what Six Sigma brings to the process, as depicted in the chart below:

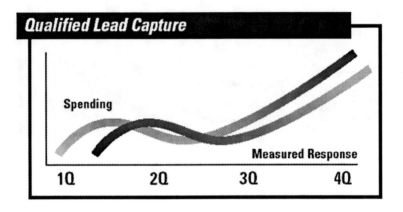

Building the name-capture process to be measured "en route," enables knowing that the target will be hit. All kinds of adjustments during the flight of the missile make it a certainty. And in the worst case scenario, if the missile is flying wildly off target, the destruct button can be used to terminate the flight without causing further damage (continually spending money on a loser property or process).

The heart of Six Sigma is the measurement in-process function. An automobile analogy once again is useful to describe this advantage.

If someone presents to me an internal combustion engine and asks me how it runs, I may be able to start it up and listen, note its odors and use other sensory perceptions to help in my assessment. If that person asks me if I thought it could be powerful enough to tow a boat, out run a car, or perform some other task, I would have to answer with, "I don't know—it sounds strong, sure looks impressive and exudes power."

Suppose that same person requested an internal combustion engine that could tow a boat, out run a car, etc. I would design and build a model to optimize the main desired function—say tow a boat. Then I would test the engine with instrumentation and measurement devices to determine to what standards to adjust the performance to achieve the specific objective. I might add a tachometer, a dynamometer, a fuel sensor, a temperature gauge—whatever would be helpful in gauging my success in building the right engine.

The same is true with Six Sigma-based sponsorship management—the sponsorship would be built to be measured in-process to ensure that the desired outcome is achieved. This design process is referred to as Design For Six Sigma—or DFSS. This design process will be discussed later.

So reducing the time lag in measured response gives us the ability to "flatten out" the spending curve and provide a predictable, return on investment scenario to consider. The following illustration points out how the Spending curve flattens out and ultimately converges with response measured in-progress.

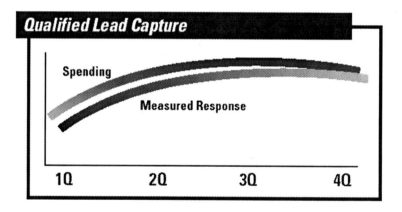

When spending starts to closely follow Measured Response, the entire relationship "quiets down" into a predictable operation that allows for efficiencies at many levels. Activation agencies can better plan with greater lead times and properties can react to changes in the activation plan.

Sponsorship Six Sigma Essential #3—Immediacy. This methodology forces thinking about how to quantify the success/failure of your relationship in immediate terms.

Thus, we not only need these long-term metrics, we also need short-term metrics—in-process checks that let us know we are on the way to the target at which we aimed.

However, most companies get away with spending money on programs with no idea of how to measure their immediate or in-process success—an activity that would get people fired in an instant in any other department of the company! Can you imagine building a new bottling plant for tens of millions of dollars and then figuring out the cost of operating it several months later in order to determine if you can market a cost competitive product?

But this is sponsorship management today. We wait a month or so to find out if sales figures went up during the big sponsorship we did in the Northeast. We wait two months to find out if our share of voice went up or down, if our unaided recall changed, etc.

It does little good to read reports weeks after an event to determine if the money invested was well spent. We want as much real-time data as possible to help maximize the efficiency and effectiveness of sponsorship spending. We want to know while the sponsorship is actually going on whether or not we are on target for success.

Advantages of using Six Sigma in Sponsorship

Process Speed and Accuracy. One of the greatest advantages of using Six Sigma in sponsorship is the inherent capacity to speed up decision-making while increasing accuracy. Let me explain these two effects.

Speed. When we have designed a sponsorship selection and management program around specific, measurable goals, it becomes much like letting a bird leave the nest, sending a child to school or launching a new business.

With Six Sigma, we have clearly defined what we expect to be the parameters for correct and responsible sponsorship decision-making. We don't need to get involved in the details—understanding if tickets are involved, what rights we have as the title sponsor, or even if the price includes crab dip at all the events. Instead, we're focused on the potential of a property to maximize the attainment of various goals.

During the actual event(s) we focus on metrics, control charts and processes. By easing the process of multiple management levels of review, we facilitate decision-making at local, regional and divisional levels based upon the stand-alone ability of the property to meet the defined and designed goals. It is less critical for corporate headquarters to review what the northwest division is considering as they now have the tools to make the decision to invest in the properties that they know will maximize their goal attainment.

Accuracy. With these clearly defined and designed goals, we are now more certain that the sponsorship decision-making at various levels in the organization will *accurately* reflect the overall goals of the company. The guessing often employed in the past can be replaced by the qualitative and quantitative assurance that investments are being made in the best available opportunities to meet goals.

The following chart demonstrates how this process interacts with several organizational realities:

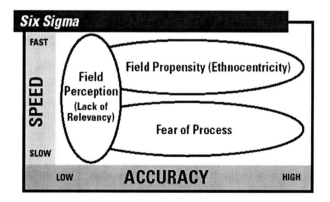

Along the vertical axis we have the variable of Speed. This is the ability of an organization to respond to an opportunity in the market place. Note that we do not advocate making quick decisions involving sponsorship investments. At the same time, we should be able to efficiently eliminate properties not in keeping with goals. The horizontal axis represents the Accuracy of a decision in meeting the goals and objectives of an organization. Let's explore some of the possible placements on this chart.

Field Propensity (**Ethnocentricity**). The first oval, aligned in an elongated fashion at the top of the chart, is labeled Field Propensity (Ethnocentricity). Ethnocentricity is a term that describes the basic human tendency to perceive one's own group as "superior." In the context of a typical sponsorship process, it is meant to characterize and validate a localized point of view. Local staff feels they can make "fast" decisions as they know "what is best for them." Because they live in the market, they are confident they have a firm grip on what their particular business needs are; who the local "players" are that need to be courted; what events warrant association, etc.

The elongation of the oval suggests lack of accuracy—the typical problem associated with this type of control. The accuracy of alignment within a decision that seeks to meet a company's overall goals (including region, division and corporation) may not be high. The field people will consider their decisions to be highly accurate—because they meet their goals and needs on at least an entertainment and hosting level. Most often these goals do not include the over-reaching goals of a region such as multicultural marketing, employee benefits and product distribution, for example. But this normally is a rather irrelevant observation to the regional person making their "fast and field accurate" decision—nothing else matters as much as their own world.

Ethnocentricity is a term used to describe a behavior centered upon one's own world and situation. Under this influence, corporate needs are not irrelevant; they are just not relevant in the sponsorship decision-making process. Hence, the accuracy of the decision could be on target with the over-arching divisional and regional goals—it may also miss these goals by a significant degree. The point is that there usually is no defined process in place to help an entire organization realize all its goals. Thus, ethnocentricity reigns.

Field Perception (**Lack of Relevancy**). The second oval is the vertical one located along the left edge of the matrix. This one is labeled Field Perception because it reflects much of what I have discovered in work with sub-headquarters organizations. Whether or not the sponsorship decision is slow or fast in its outcome, it will be highly inaccurate in the opinion of the Field. The field often sees headquarters decisions as being "out of touch" with their particular needs or situation. Thus the decision will lack any relevancy to the field and the view that "headquarters has no idea what it is we are trying to do out here" prevails. A typical result is that the field has little or no enthusiasm for the corporate sponsorship.

Fear of Process. The last oval, located along the bottom edge of the matrix is labeled Fear of Process. Whether or not the accuracy of a sponsorship decision-making process is low or high, one thing is certain—the Field believes it will incur unacceptable delay. Thus, an often-heard rationale is, "We'll miss many opportunities because of this slowness. It is better to quickly react to the offer and get the good deal than to be accurate across all organization boundaries." We could say that installing a process of sponsorship decision-making instills "fear" among the troops because, according to popular belief, everything takes *forever* at corporate, right?

All three of these undesirable outcomes are the product of lack of organization and communication as to how sponsorship should be managed. If we were to look at the same organization that lacks process control in sponsorship, we would often find a highly defined (if not over-defined) process for capital equipment requests and approvals. The decision to buy a $100,000 piece of factory equipment is not a whimsical affair to be made by one person who thinks they need more technology or better machinery. Not at all—these $100,000-level decisions need to be carefully thought through and calculated against the return on the investment they will require.

The opposite is true with many organizations when it comes to sponsorship. A sponsorship decision involving more than $100,000 often is made without the discernment and inspection given other purchases of half that amount. Thus, the process becomes slow or inaccurate and succumbs to the outcomes listed above.

TAKE-AWAY

With a Six Sigma-based process, we have the ability to be both quick in decision-making (because it can function in a highly decentralized way) and accurate in achieving over-reaching company objectives.

Decision-making Toolkits, often consisting of a high-level qualitative questionnaire that helps determine if an opportunity should be explored and a second-level, quantitative questionnaire designed to determine if an opportunity is well-aligned with business goals, facilitate decentralization. The second-level analysis usually includes the weighting of goals and objectives to determine the closeness of "fit," thus supporting data-driven decisions. These tools help sub-headquarters personnel make decisions that are good for them, the division and the company overall.

Rather than fearing corporate interference or inordinate delays in the process, the field personnel find themselves empowered by the Six Sigma approach, able to make sponsorship decisions with relative speed and confidence.

Recalling the Vision of Leadership graphic from Chapter 2, we see that occupying a place in the highly coveted "Controlled Investments" area of the matrix is possible.

4

Application of Six Sigma

GOALS DRIVE THE SPONSORSHIP SELECTION PROCESS

Most sponsorship relationships today start with the property and/or its sales agents approaching large corporations with a "package." They have a set of prices and benefits associated with differing levels of sponsorship. These may include:

1. Tickets

2. Suites

3. Passes

4. Production days

5. Appearances, etc.

The property develops a tiered structure that matches more of the above perks against additional money/resources/in-kind.

Business goals supersede all others. In contrast, with Six Sigma, we start by determining what the sponsor is trying to achieve in business—not only in marketing and definitely not solely in sponsorship. Ideally, a complete understanding of what the sponsor is trying to achieve in the marketplace. Sponsorship can be used to accomplish many non-traditional marketing objectives. Let's take a look at just one example: employee retention.

If a company has a program designed for employee retention, it will most likely be administered by the HR department and involve gifts, training, financial incentives, etc. In addition, other programs such as internal communications may be administered by the PR group. Their mandate centers around getting the great news out about how well the company is doing and how much the company values its employees.

The marketing department might not have any sort of employee objectives built into their plans. Any why should they?—This is an HR or PR function.

But with sponsorship, an entire investment can be built around this one non-traditional marketing objective. Employee turnover can cost a company thousands and thousands of dollars in recruitment fees, interviewing times, expenses involving bringing recruits for interviews, training, etc. A modest investment in a sponsorship that connects with employees' passions can be leveraged into multi-faceted programs designed to inspire and motivate them.

Take-a-Note: I know of one company that justified its entire $1-million plus investment in NASCAR for this one employee goal. The fact that they also used it for customer entertainment was entirely secondary. The point is, working from normal sponsorship goals, one would never know to design the relationship around this important non-marketing goal. Thus, understanding all the business goals of the sponsor from the start of the engagement is imperative. This is a dramatic example of the power of Six Sigma in realizing company objectives through sponsorship.

Once all goals are understood, a process can be applied to distill these large company-level goals down to actionable and measurable sponsorship activities in a process referred to as "Y" Discernment. More on the Y Discernment process later in this book. Thus an understanding between sponsor and property can be created that addresses the needs to create a mutually profitable relationship.

Knowing the goals allows approaching the property with a set of objectives that must be realized in the course of the relationship. We are not concerned with what perks or other compensation the property has to offer. We are concerned with how the property can help realize business goals.

The sponsor's needs in the relationship are now clearly understood—but we must use the fundamental design methodology of Six Sigma in order to realize the full potential of the goals. Thus, we **D**efine, **M**easure, **A**nalyze, **I**mprove and **C**ontrol sponsorship programs for maximum return and efficiency. This will be the focus for the remainder of this book.

When the relationship is designed in this way, that is, to be measured, all the other components and attendant benefits of Six Sigma fall naturally into place. Most important will be the use of analysis, improvement and control. The key takeaway here is that instead of accepting a property's standard package of costs, start with fundamental questions: the business goals, the marketing goals and how the sponsorship can be used via different kind of properties (whether sports, not-for-profit, cause-related, entertainment, industry events, trade shows, arts, etc.) to best meet those goals.

MEASUREMENT

Six Sigma provides the observer with data to determine if a process is in control. The control that most companies seek in using Six Sigma is in both return on investment and in cost control. Let's start with what ROI means to many companies.

Return on Investment (ROI). ROI is normally defined as the return in monetary benefit on a given investment. The "return" is the numerator and the "investment" is the denominator. Put in simple mathematical form, this is depicted as:

Return on Investment = Return divided by Investment

While this formula looks deceptively simple, the actual process of determining ROI can be difficult. Because so few companies build sponsorship around (Y-Discerned) company objectives, it is very difficult to calculate a true return. Return often is calculated using the field sales people's best estimates. In one large study we conducted, the directly attributed sales figures connected to the sponsorship provided by the client actually turned out to be the opinion of a veteran field salesman who gave his best estimate of what percentage of the company's sales would be at risk if they gave up the long-standing relationship.

When sponsorship is designed (or redesigned for existing sponsorship relationships) from the beginning to be measured, it is relatively simple to put the measurement devices and procedures in place to understand the return, often on a real-time basis.

The same is true with investment. The true cost of investment often is not included in the ROI that many companies attempt to calculate. Investment should include items more far-reaching than just the direct cost of the sponsorship property. An abbreviated list of investment categories might include:

Direct payment to property for sponsorship rights (whatever this entails)

Activation cost to leverage the property:

> On-site marketing activities, such as product displays, sampling, data capture, etc.
> VIP entertainment
> Flights
> Accommodations
> Tickets (rarely included in the sponsorship deal)
> Parking
> Transportation
> Meals
> Management time (planning, attending, following up)

Partnership costs with other sponsors
Advertising to support the sponsorship
Public relations

Understanding the true return and investment is vastly easier and much more accurate when the relationship with the property is clearly defined up front. It is vital to remember that the definitions must be provided by the sponsor, not the property.

Rationalization of Alternatives. There are many tools used in business today to choose between alternative demands for scarce resources. Some of the common business decision tools include: Net Present Value (NPV), Internal Rate of Return (IRR), and the previously described Return on Investment (ROI). All these tools attempt to bring facts and data into decision-making. I won't go into detail on all of these tools. I only mention them to draw the clear analogy on how this Six Sigma approach to sponsorship recognizes and intentionally builds upon this inherent management practice and philosophy of using analysis to support large investment decisions.

A significant refinement in the development of this decision-making bag of tools is the Z Score. This is the tool that allows the Six Sigma sponsorship practitioner to compare competing investment options across many segments and properties.

The Z Score. The Z Score can be a difficult concept for the novice to Six Sigma. Simply put, the Z Score is a numerical rating for the efficiency of a process in meeting a goal. We will explore the actual mathematical construction below, but for now, it is vital that the reader understands philosophically what a Z Score means. We will also assume that the reader has a basic familiarity with the concept of the Normal Distribution which we discuss in detail below as well.

The Z Score is the fundamental metric to measure and maximize efficiency of spending; it reflects the efficiency of a process in achieving its objective. Let's start with an explanation of what exactly the Z Score is and how we calculate it.

The Z Score is a statistic that relates the efficiency of any process in reaching a closely defined objective. The Z Score is "dimensionless." This refers to the fact that it doesn't relate to any specific dimensional metric. It's unlike many other comparative metrics that use a base measurement standard to understand the relationships involved.

The Z Score reveals how well a process is meeting its intended goal. A very low Z Score (perhaps a 1 or even a negative number in some applications) indicates that the variability in the process is so high that the reliability of meeting the goal is low. Conversely, a very high Z Score (perhaps a 4 or even a 6), indicates that the variability in the process is so low that the reliability of meeting the goal is high. Confidence in the process to meet the goal is warranted.

Let's look at an example. If a repetitive process such as pan-European promotion of a product with a goal of 1,000 consumer trials at each stop on the tour is under study, the ability of the activities designed to meet that goal of 1,000 trials can be measured. Efficiency may be reflected by a Z Score of "2."

Without going into the statistical details of what this means in terms of expected results and standard deviation, suffice it to say that on a standard scale of 0 to 6 in Z Score or process efficiency, a 2 would not be considered outstanding. However, without comparative data, it couldn't be known if a 2 is the best score due to "noise" (see Take-a-Note below) and other uncontrollable variables. On the other hand, if we calculated a Z Score of 5 we could be relatively confident that our process is very much in control and capable of meeting the goal we have established for that process. Later we will explore how to improve this score and maximize our return on this investment.

What the Z Score can and cannot measure. The power of Z Scores is undeniable. However, it must be remembered that the power lies in process repeatability. I recommend that Z Scores only be used under the following conditions:

1. The process or program has repetitive elements (with well-defined goals!) and the data can be reliably acquired. DO NOT use this tool with singular events like one concert event or one art show.

2. A certified Six Sigma black belt can confidently affirm the significance of the data and the process goals. If your organization doesn't have a black belt, make sure your sponsorship agency does. We will explain the concept of "belts" later in the book.

3. The measured process has a statistically significant amount of iterations to allow for the process to pass standard tests of normality of data (again, this is why you will want to follow condition 1 above).

4. The effort will result in a set of data that will be of use to the company. This may sound a little obvious, but too often a company will calculate data for the sake of calculating data. If there are no alternatives with which to compare the efficiency of this process, then the calculation of the Z Score may not be vital in the decision making process of distributing scarce resources.

Thus, the Z Score can measure processes that are repetitive and have objectives. Some examples would include:

Sales events over a period of time (an 8-week campaign)
Concert tours
Consumer data capture at a series of sporting events (baseball season)
Entertainment of clients at golf events over a season

The Z Score cannot measure those processes that are not often repeated or do not have an objective. Examples would include:

The Super Bowl in the NFL—event is too infrequent
One-time promotion events such as a July 4th sales event

Any sponsorship that does not have a measurable objective, such as a major sports team sponsorship without objectives

The fact that some processes cannot be understood from a process efficiency view, or a Z Score, perspective does not mean they are not good investments for sponsorship. If you refer to the Pyramid of Enlightenment section of the book, this can be a natural stepping off point for many sponsorships.

It is important to note that the inability to compute a Z Score also does not mean the process should not be subjected to strict objective development and Six Sigma-based analysis.

The Z Score doesn't have a metric comparison. It is not miles per gallon, cost per thousand, cents per pound, liters per hour, etc. It is simply the ability of the process to achieve a stated objective. Let's look at how the Z Score is calculated.

$$Z = (\text{Objective} - \text{Mean}) / \text{Standard Deviation}$$
-or-
$$Z = (\text{Mean} - \text{Objective}) / \text{Standard Deviation}$$

The reason there are two formulae is because our purpose may better be served by achieving either a higher metric or a lower one. For instance, demonstrating the attainment of a higher metric when measuring a process' ability to increase the number of names acquired during an event may be the desire. Conversely, reaching a lower metric when attempting to lower the cost of acquisition per prospect name may be the aim.

The important thing to note in the calculation is what should be recognized from a process standpoint. Let's examine the numerator first.

Z SCORE EXAMPLE: ATTRACTION EVENT

In this example we will use the first form: Objective minus Mean. Situation: We are sponsoring an event in which one goal is to maximize potential customer visits to our display area at the event.

The objective, based upon previous experience, is set at drawing 1,000 people. Objectives such as this often are based upon expectations of both the client and our agency expertise. This is a form of "base-lining" which is very helpful in setting up initial Six Sigma programs.

Let's assume that after five events, we have the following set of customer visit data: 900; 800; 1,000; 700; and 600.

To obtain the mean for our numerator, we sum the data set and divide by the number of points of data:

Sum of data = 4,000
Number of data points = 5 (900, 800, 1,000, 700, 600)
Mean = 4,000/5 = 800

This means, on average, the "attraction event" as we have been conducting it will draw 800 people to our next similarly designed event.

What does this mean or average tell us? Five separate events were staged, all attracting differing amounts of people—ranging from a great event with 1,000 attractions and a less stellar event with only 600 people. Without knowing the specifics of each event, we cannot speculate on why one was more successful than the other. Perhaps weather affected the attendance, or the events were held on different days of the week, or in different regions of the country where the property was more or less popular, etc.

Take-a-Note: The impact of noise on data

A key takeaway from the Attraction Event example is a concept commonly referred to as "noise." Noise in a set of data refers to variables that are affecting the data or results of what is being measured. Some environmental "noise" fac-

tors were listed above. Weather normally is considered to be "uncontrolled noise." That is, we cannot control the weather in any direct sense. At the same time, we can do many things to ameliorate the effect of the noise—reducing the effect of the variable on the event. In the case of weather, perhaps this means we need to be located indoors to attract people, which may be more expensive and require more coordination. Examples of controllable noise include: who works the attraction event (the event management company, the specific people, perhaps) and how people are attracted (visuals, aural stimulation, incentives, etc.).

Quick point—there's a measurement trap to be avoided here: we have to temper our desire to maintain too-rigid an event design consistency. True, that will help ensure fair comparison of events while eliminating or at least reducing the noise inherent in event management. However, we may be given an opportunity to relocate from a poor position in a distant part of the main event, to a location right next door to the entrance. I would not advocate turning down the superior positioning at the expense of the client for the sake of gathering consistent data. We must remember to be practical in our application of methodology.

The reason it is so important to understand the impact of noise on data is because it is a VERY REAL aspect of Six Sigma-based marketing. In Six Sigma's traditional applications, the variables are usually much more controllable. They include an order being taken inaccurately, a different technician finishing a job than started it, time of day, the supplier of stock material, etc. In marketing through sponsorship, we are operating in a very fluid environment dominated by the human interaction that is at the core of our version of this unique communication channel. This point is critical to understand when explaining, designing, analyzing and presenting our commercial version of Six Sigma.

In fact, it may be readily expected to be the major argument from the skeptics of this method. They may cite the noise factors as so important as to make analysis inaccurate. This is not the case at all. Six Sigma is a better way to manage business because it uses data and facts to drive better solutions. Even so, keep the following in mind: we are not discounting variances inherent in human behavior nor are we advocating a strict interpretation of the data and the resulting analysis. We are providing a guide—or tool—not dissimilar to Net Present Value, to aid the sponsorship decision maker.

So returning to our example of the attraction event, we know our average or mean level of attraction over the past five events has been 800 people. This is well short of our stated objective of 1,000 people. Recall the calculation of the numerator:

(Objective—Mean) = (1,000—800) = 200

Let's now turn our attention to the bottom (denominator) number—the standard deviation. If we parse the term we can understand the components fairly easily:

Standard—the central average or mean

Deviation—how much the data deviates from the central average or mean.

In essence, we are calculating the amount the data deviates or varies from the central mean. What good does this number do us in our understanding of the data? It is vital to our understanding of how well the process is duplicating itself. Let's look at Graph A to illustrate this point:

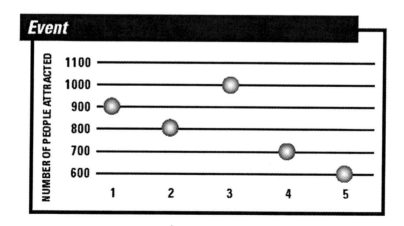

Looking at the data, we see that the difference or variance between event 1 and event 2 is only 100 people. But the difference or variance between event 3 and event 4 is 300 people. The variance is dramatically different between those two events.

The standard deviation is a statistical tool to tell us how much variance we have in our data. Let's consider two extreme examples:

If we had collected data on the five events and the results had very little variance between points, we would have a nearly straight line across Graph B as illustrated below:

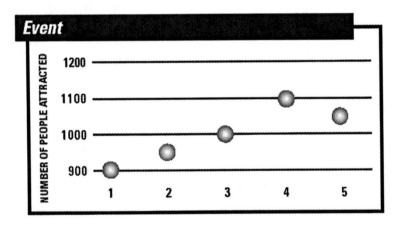

The single largest variance we can identify is between event 3 and 4, and that is only 100 people. In every other instance, the variance is only 50 people from one event to the next.

If we had collected data from the five different events and the data points were wildly different, the data would look like Graph C:

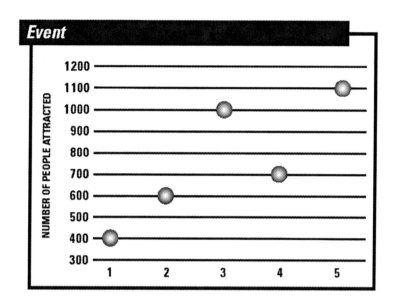

Here, there is really no discernable pattern. The data plots are all over the chart. The variance between data points is large.

The standard deviation is nothing more than further calculation of the variance between the different data points. Now instead of considering how much the data varies from one point to the next, we are concerned with how much the data varies from the central mean. This formula is a quick diagnostic tool statisticians use to understand how much each point used in the data set varies from the mean value. Why is this important?

The greater the variance from the mean, the more unpredictable the next occurrence in the data set will be. Imagine how important the need for controlling the variance is in the case of an anticipated bullet trajectory. If the variance was great between each data point or bullet, we would have no idea of where the bullet might land. The same is true with aircraft navigation, missile guidance, laser eye surgery, etc.

Let's look at a graphic depiction of standard deviation in Graph D below.

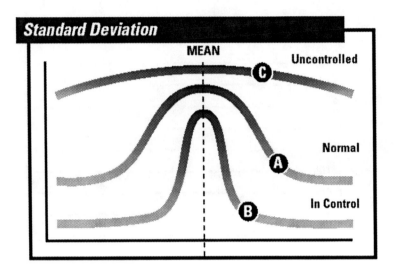

Relative to the normal bell curve distribution (A), once can easily see that the tightly controlled process characterized by (B) has very little deviation from the mean. We can expect results in this controlled process to be fairly predictable within a small range of values depicted by the x-axis. The uncontrolled process (C), has relatively high deviation from the mean, making accurate prediction of future results difficult. In Six Sigma, the aim is to reduce deviation and create a tightly controlled process as depicted by B in the graph.

This need for control over variance drives Six Sigma and its application to continuous process improvement. The lower the variance in the data, the more assurance there is of similar and repeated results.

Let's consider the data from Graph A. The average (mean) calculated out at 800 people. The data group didn't look all that close to one another and the associated standard deviation calculated out at 141 people.

In Graph B, the average is 1,000 and the standard deviation calculated out at only 71 people.

In Graph C, the average is 760 and the standard deviation is 258 people.

This tells us quite a bit about the rough outcome of our five events. But it doesn't tell us how CONSISTENT the results were at all. Our first example is nearly twice as dispersed or variable as our second example (141 people in standard deviation versus 71 people). However, our last example is nearly twice as dispersed or variable as our first example.

The conclusion, based upon the data, would be that the first example is much more stable—or predicable—at reproducing the expected average or mean of attracting 800 people than our last example. However, the second example is even better at reproducing the expected average or mean as our first example.

So now we have our standard deviation—our bottom (denominator) number to complete the equation:

Z Score = (Objective—Mean)/Standard Deviation
Z Score = 800/141
Z Score = 5.67

The Z Score of 5.67 is an indicator of fairly high process control in achieving the goal as currently set in the equation.

So what can we conclude? Without another example with which to compare, we are limited to describing the efficiency of the process in achieving the objective of attracting 1,000 people.

As discussed above, this is a good time to review the Normal Distribution.

NORMAL DISTRIBUTION

The validity of our standard deviation accuracy is highly dependent upon the data being normal in distribution. Briefly, a set of data that is normal in distribution means that it follows a highly repetitive and identifiable pattern of results.

A rigorous statistical explanation of this process isn't necessary but a high-level overview of the effects and inherent implications in a Normal Distribution is needed for the reader to understand the foundation statistic of Six Sigma.

If an event is conducted in sufficient repetitions, the tendency of most objects toward the average result will be observed. In the first example, we calculated 800 as the average result. If we repeated this process over and over again, we might observe that the result will be greater than 800 some of the time and less than 800 other times. More than likely, that result will "straddle" the mean result of 800 with an equal number of events occurring above the 800 average and an equal amount occurring below the average.

This is essentially the Normal Distribution. Its shape gives it the nickname bell curve that is a staple of grammar school grade reporting (fitting the curve).

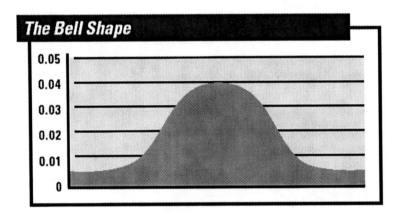

The Bell Shape

Not all things in nature will follow this distribution pattern. There are many tests in statistics used to understand or verify if, indeed, the data are normal. Leave this to a Six Sigma Green (part-time Six Sigma expert) or Black Belt (full-time Six Sigma expert). For our purposes, we will assume the data are normal as the vast majority of natural events fall easily under this definition.

Take-a-note: Six Sigma Green Belts and Black Belts

Most organizations deploying Six Sigma as an essential management tool have an established hierarchy for training and advancing people involved in the Six Sigma process. While there are many variants, they share a few common characteristics:

1. *Being trained in Six Sigma is not an option—it is an imperative. This is the case with many leading companies.*

2. *In order to advance within the organization, you must spend time in a Six Sigma leadership role (Black Belt position explained below).*

3. *Six Sigma "language" or terms are used throughout the management culture.*

Most also have an established "rank" to identify what level of Six Sigma a person has been certified.

1. *Black Belt. This designation is for those people who have a job totally designed around delivering on Six Sigma project initiatives. They may or may not actually run projects themselves, as they are often mentoring man, Green Belts at once on their individual projects. Some organizations have a "Master Black Belt" classification—this is the person in charge of the other Black Belts' development and project deliverables.*

2. *Green Belt. This designation is similar to a Black Belt, with the very important distinction that the person holding a Green Belt will also be employed full time in another role/job. In the case of many leading companies, most general managers are Green Belts, performing both functions. The level of training is identical to that of a Black Belt—they are just not dedicated solely to Six Sigma goals. Green Belt certification usually entails two weeks of intense training followed by the completion of two certifying projects within a year of training completion. Most Green Belts are expected to be working on two projects at any given time—while closing at least one to two projects out per year.*

3. *Yellow Belt. This designation is for those people who have been famil-
    iarized with Six Sigma and may have some exposure in their everyday
    jobs to the company's efforts. In some very large companies, this is the
    level of training most employees receive. It normally entails several
    days of training and may or may not involve a certification process
    that includes completing one or more projects.*

*While all belt designations play a function within a company's overall Six
Sigma goals, you should not expect a Yellow Belt to understand the complexi-
ties of a complete Six Sigma program.*

So what do we know about the Normal Distribution? For one thing, it is
unique to a set of data. The resulting bell shape is either more flat in
appearance or more steep or vertical. The more dispersed the data, the flat-
ter the curve. The tighter the data to each other, the more vertical the
curve.

The most important understanding of our use of the Normal Distribution
is what it tells us about the probability of the result of the next iteration in
our continued observance of the process.

When data sets are normal, the statistical probability of the next observed
data point landing somewhere in the range of the average/mean, plus or
minus one standard deviation, is 68 percent.

Using our attraction example, we could say that the next event will most
likely fall (68 percent of the time, we expect) between the average of 800
plus or minus the standard deviation of 141 people. This would produce a
range of:

800 - 141 = 659
800 + 141 = 941
659————————Next result————————941

Thus, two-thirds of the time, we expect the next occurrence to land in this
range. But what about the other one-third of the time?

If we extend out our coverage to the mean plus or minus two standard deviations, we could say that the next event will fall (95 percent of the time, say the statisticians) between the average of 800 plus or minus two standard deviations of 141 people. This would produce a much wider range of:

800 - (2 x 141) = 800 - 282 = 518
800 + (2 x 141) = 800 + 282 = 1082
518————————Next result————————1082

As observed, this is a much higher range—if you will, a much "easier" target to hit. The bull's eye on the target has gotten much larger. The expected result is not different—just our calculation of the probability of that result landing in a larger range of possible values.

This process of widening the range will lead to an eventual calculation of an expected confidence value of 99.9997 percent—that is Six Sigma—or an expected result that is within six standard deviations of the mean.

Differing levels of Six Sigma attainment can be illustrated in terms of failures to meet the expected result as follows:

1 Sigma—690,000
2 Sigma—308,537
3 Sigma—66,807
4 Sigma—6,210
5 Sigma—233
6 Sigma—3.4

So, with a process that is "in control" with Six Sigma accuracy, we will only have 3.4 "failures" to meet our goal in one million operations! That sounds like an unbelievable level of quality in achieving a goal in a process—until we consider what level airlines operate at.

Let's assume that the global airline industry completes 2.25 million flights per month. If the airline industry was to perform at 6 Sigma (e.g. no crash), we would have nearly 7 airline crashes per month! That's hardly acceptable.

So let's return to the example where our result was a Z Score of 5.67.

There are three numbers in this equation—the mean, the standard deviation and the goal. How do we control these factors to raise the efficiency of the process of attracting people to our display/event?

Mean. We can adjust the average number of people that we attract. This can be done in a variety of ways. I assure you the visitor number would skyrocket if we advertised that each person coming to our attraction event display area would receive $100! In this case, the mean would move up considerably—as would the total event cost to the client—which would make the ROI drop like a rock. So we will use Design of Experiments (see Chapter 7—DOEs) to test more economical ways of raising the mean without spending more money.

Standard Deviation. We can affect the standard deviation of the number of people attracted by developing a more controlled process—taking out the noise discussed earlier. Often, this costs money. To eliminate noise, we may need a better location out of the weather, the same or even higher quality and more experienced people working the event, better graphics, etc. Using DOE, we will also test ways of better reducing the standard deviation without spending significantly more money.

The Goal. The goal can be changed and that will dramatically affect the Z Score of the process. Why and when should we adjust the goal? If we are achieving Z Scores in excess of 4 we should immediately consider setting a more aggressive goal. The actual goal is less important than its consistent application across sponsorship activity comparisons.

The most important application of the Z Score is to use it in comparing the proverbial "apples to oranges." Since the Z Score is the fundamental metric to measure and maximize efficiency of spending, I often use this common analogy to explain how we use it to compare seemingly incomparable sponsorship properties. Our Six Sigma process provides a clear way of changing this situation.

And you probably are thinking the same thing right now: How is it possible to compare football to the ballet to the art exhibit to the local baseball team? Answer: By using the Z Score of the efficiency of the investment.

Z SCORE COMPARISON

To drill down on this, take the example shown below:

Segment	Property	Y	Goal	Z
Sports	PGA	Employee Retention	85% Participation	1.5
Art	Monet Exhibit	Name Capture	$5 Per Name	2.0
Entertainment	Rolling Stones Tour	Product Demo	500 Trials Per Concert	3.0

If a client is using differing types (apples & oranges) of sponsorships to achieve the goal of attracting potential consumers, an examination of which segment or particular property is most efficient in its ability to accomplish the goal can be conducted. As previously mentioned, it is important in comparing efficiencies of differing properties to use the same goal in the calculation of the Z Score.

More importantly, we can also use the Z Score to compare investment efficiencies in properties that are being used to achieve differing goals. This is the true power in the application of Six Sigma in the world of marketing in general and sponsorship in particular. Here we see that the Entertainment segment with a Z of 3.0 is the most efficient of the segments compared.

By using this process to set up sponsorships that can be measured against certain goals, we can build a client's property base with inherent measurement capability. It now is possible to determine that using golf for customer entertainment is more efficient than sponsoring an art exhibit for new customer attraction.

Take-a-Note: Honesty is the best policy

A word of caution: When comparing differing goals, we have to strongly encourage the client to be as honest as possible in goal setting. Why? It's easy to manipulate the goal, and thus the Z Score. If the client makes the goal too easy, this will most definitely skew the result to achieve a high Z Score.

Let's take a hypothetical client that loves golf and hates art. Such a client can make the golf goals easy and the art goals difficult (so long as they are not comparing like goals, such as new customer attraction across both properties—in which case it would not be possible to cheat).

The important point is that if this is the case, it indicates the client has little interest in actually achieving efficiencies or rationalizing their property base, so the chances of a successful engagement are very slim from the outset. Using Six Sigma to distinguish which investment is more efficient will not help in this situation.

If, however, the client is capable of being honest in goal setting and evaluation (and subsequent adjustment) of their Z Score results, this tool can be as valuable as any other major financial decision making tool (such as the NPV or IRR calculations).

Thus, the PRISM Six Sigma Z Score provides the client with the ability to compare apples to oranges. This is a simple concept if you think about how one would compare apples to oranges in a daily situation. They both have differing weights that are entirely comparable; they both have differing caloric content that are entirely comparable; the possibilities are numerous.

Testing Alternatives. Another tremendous application of this process is the ability to help the client test alternative investments prior to making any major decisions. We have the ability to design the process in lieu of mass investment. Remember, most sponsorship investments today are done without any real up-front investment analysis. Thus, clients are presented with million-dollar decisions under the premise of branding, brand awareness, brand association, etc. with little advance analysis.

TAKE-AWAY

This chapter has provided a clear understanding of a rigorous analytical approach to sponsorship management. Business (and thus brand) goals must lead all sponsorship investment success criteria. We cannot rely upon the disconnected common package offer from properties to help achieve business goals. We must form the clay to our specific vision. This is done by working with the properties to jointly deliver on these important objectives. Six Sigma forges the linkage to make these mutually supporting relationships successful. In many instances, we can use Z Scores to help determine where our investments are most efficiently returning our capital.

Some properties will resist this more rigorous approach; it exposes them to measurement and performance. The good properties will cooperate and welcome this new wave of thinking for three good reasons:

1. They will have proof for the sponsor that the property delivers on the promises to meet business goals of the investing sponsor. This will enable them to ask for even more money!

2. They will be able to use the results to sell other sponsors on the efficacy of their offer.

3. They will learn how to make their property even better through efficiencies, thereby reducing or stopping counterproductive activities and programs that don't add value and actually increase their own costs of servicing the client.

The Holy Grail. We now have the ability to understand investments and make rational business decisions on how to invest resources.

5

Connecting Business Goals to Sponsorship

The ways in which companies may begin a Six Sigma-based initiative can be as varied as the companies themselves. They range from transforming an entire business to making strategic improvements in the company's marketing program to narrowly focused problem-solving. In Sponsorship Six Sigma, I generally view the application in broad terms as either a Strategic Review or an Audit/Analysis.

For instance, if an analysis of a whole segment of sponsorship such as Industry Events were to be undertaken against a company's Business Goals, we could call that a Strategic Review. On the other hand, if we were to analyze a specific sponsorship, say an art exhibition supported by the company, again, against Business Goals, that would fall into the Audit category. Why is a distinction necessary? It's useful to bear in mind that the more narrowly focused Audit approach may not lead to a Strategic Review.

Let me make it clear that in nearly all cases, an Audit **should** lead to a Strategic Review. A complete and accurate audit necessitates a clear understanding of the business goals that comprise the foundation of a Strategic Review. However, it has been my experience that some clients eschew the Strategic Review for the instant gratification of an Audit. Let's explore the various factors that relate to this "strategic review avoidance" problem.

1. Business goals simply aren't known. Oftentimes, sponsorship falls under the purview of marketing, sales or public relations depart-

ments. Depending on the size of the company, this may explain two common reasons for the apparent ignorance.

    a. Not senior enough. The project manager may not be senior enough, or vested with sufficient "line of sight" in the organization to have visibility of these goals.

    b. Not clearly communicated through organization

2. The costs of the larger study are constrained by budget

3. Urgency—too pressed for time to consider a larger study

    a. Specific property negotiations are starting very soon

    b. More senior people want an answer to the pressing question of value and it's surmised that an approach for a larger study wouldn't be well received.

Having identified why a Strategic Review might be foregone, we need to address the different ways to temper this problem.

1. Find the information on strategic and tactical business objectives yourself.

    a. Researching readily available public sources of information (internet search)

    b. SEC filings

    c. Ask the advertising agency—an important partner in this process

2. Conduct the analysis without the Strategic Review framework

    a. Determine only a monetary ROI for the property in question

    b. Forego the important question of the true appropriateness of a property for the company

    c. Leverage initial study into a presentation highlighting the inherent need for further analysis against actual business goals.

It's possible that only one program needs reformation. But if we begin by committing to a Strategic Review, this inevitably will lead to the Audit of sponsored activities—unless a company has never sponsored at all. This would be a rare find, indeed.

Motivation aside…Regardless of how and why the approach is introduced to the organization, we'll conclude by recalling the three fundamental keys to all Six Sigma sponsorship strategies:

1.   The need to understand the company's specific business goals.

2.   The need to be able to measure progress toward achieving the goals.

3.   The immediacy, or short term, metric requirement that demonstrates that progress is being made to successfully achieve the goals identified in the processes of numbers 1 and 2.

This sounds deceptively simple. But goals often are characterized very broadly—such as "getting more business."

Nearly all such goals can be walked through a simple process that breaks down broad goals into understandable and realizable business objectives. The tools I have developed will help make sense of the most common marketing goals or objectives. The first tool is what I call the Five Questions.

The five questions for all sponsorship investments are as follows—and by the way, these questions apply to both current and prospective relationships.

THE FIVE QUESTIONS

1.   As the sponsorship relationship currently exists, what business goal(s) DOES the sponsorship seek to affect?

2.   In an ideal relationship with the property, what business goal(s) COULD the sponsorship really affect? In other words, could the sponsorship be made to affect these goals?

3. How does one know the goal is being affected—how does one know success is being achieved?

4. How does one measure the long term performance of achieving the goal?

5. How does one measure the short term (in-process) achievement of the goal?

Let's take an example of this line of questioning. Suppose a sponsor had a goal of "more business." In examining if a current sponsored property had the ability to deliver on that goal, the Five Questions would be asked. As an example, an existing golf tournament sponsorship will be used as the property in question.

1. What business goal(s) does the sponsorship seek to affect? How does the golf tournament help the sponsor achieve the goal of generating more business?

The first wall of the questioning process has arisen. What does "more business" really mean? How can this be expressed in goal-oriented, realizable terms? This requires the second main tool needed to connect business goals to sponsorship—Y Discernment. Recall the equation from earlier in this book, $Y = f(x)$. Y Discernment facilitates understanding of what the sponsorship goals (Y's) really mean—and how those goals can be affected, influenced or achieved by the use of sponsorship. For now, let's say that the goal of more business is defined as entertaining potential customers in a pleasant setting. Many will recognize this line of reasoning from the experience of watching companies getting involved in sponsorship.

So we will assume it does affect this one goal of more business. But remember, sponsors will have many, many business goals spanning lots of different aspects of their operations. This question will be repeated for every goal—which is why we need to understand what the goals really mean and how sponsorship could be used to achieve them. On to question 2:

2.   In an ideal relationship with the property, what business goal(s) COULD the sponsorship really affect? In other words, could the sponsorship be made to affect these goals? We already have identified one sub goal of more business above, namely as entertaining potential customers in a pleasant setting. What other business goals could the golf sponsorship affect? Let's use an often overlooked, yet highly valuable use of sponsorships—the internal employee reward or incentive. We will assume that the company desires to keep its high-performing employees and would like to provide additional perks to motivate and reward them. Without going into details of what employee performance parameters would be set to meet the eligibility for this reward (attendance, sales goals, etc.), we can easily see that the golf sponsorship could be modified to address this valuable additional goal. This may be the case for many, many more company goals—which we may not discover if we are not conducting a Strategic Review.

3.   How does one know the goal is being affected—how to know success is being achieved? This can stump the person who does not have a rigorous plan—they may never have thought about their goal beyond just the simple goal of more business. Many sponsors will just assume more business is measured by the sales force as number of new prospective clients brought to the golf tournament. Answers can be very broad at this point. Using the golf tournament example, we could say that if the goal is more business, we know it is being affected by how much new or incremental business is being generated from the people we invite to the golf tournaments. However, the next two questions will drive home the point that this simply is not enough.

4.   How does one measure the long-term performance of achieving the goal? The common metrics will come out immedi-

ately—sales go up! Market share, share of voice, etc., all increase in some fashion. Record these goals in the plan—they are vitally important—particularly if a major advertising agency is involved as a partner, because these are the measures of the agency's very existence. But remember from the earlier discussion, this is a historical analysis. It doesn't reveal in-process if the goal was being achieved. It's simply a school grade at the end of a semester, A or B or worse. There have been no mid-term exams or interim grades to indicate a D was in the making—all that is known is a horrible job was done. Thus, the need for question 5.

5.   How then, to measure the short term (in-process) progress toward achieving the goal? This is a critical question for the Six Sigma process. In fact, it may be nearly impossible to achieve progress without this aspect of extrapolating business goals to sponsorship. We simply must know if we are heading toward the bull's eye. Using our example of the golf tournament, we need to develop ways to measure in-progress whether or not the path toward achieving the long-term goal is being followed.

Let's assume that using the golf tournament to entertain customers involves the critical step of inviting certain key people to the event. One short-term measurement could be the ratio of actual attendees to total invitations—in essence, how attractive was the invitation to the sponsored event? This can be taken one step further and defined as the ratio of desired attendees to those who actually showed up. Why the difference? Because a purchasing agent may have been invited to the tournament and he or she may have passed the tickets along to the receptionist. This refinement deals with the quality of the attendee versus the number of attendees—an important distinction, I think you will agree, when the whole goal is to influence decision-makers.

Use of the Five Questions has addressed the three fundamental requirements for a successful property selection and sponsorship strategy design: understanding the goals; agreement on what comprises successful progress toward the goals; and the appropriate long-term and short-term metrics to verify progress.

During the questioning process, the fundamental blocks for a solid new goal- and results-oriented sponsorship investment also have been built.

TOOL KIT DEVELOPMENT

Based on this fundamental understanding of the sponsorship and what it hopes to achieve in a business sense, an analytic tool can be developed to assure consistency and help to guide the process to success. This tool can be further refined into a two-part sponsorship tool kit. While large corporations already use tool kits in many activities to ensure compliance or uniformity of process, we recommend the two-stage tool kit process in the review of sponsorships.

Stage I. The first stage consists of a high-level qualitative questionnaire that provides a quick screening to determine if an opportunity/property should be explored in depth. This Stage I analysis can take the form of a simple series of questions, which address the property's compatibility with a company's (business unit or region, etc.) business goals. Each question elicits a pass-fail answer, and an overall score is tallied at the end. When a sponsorship marketing professional who has been trained in this process subjects a property to this type of honest, business-based probing—often no more than 10 or 12 questions—it quickly becomes apparent if the sponsorship deserves further consideration. Most, of course, won't make it past this stage. Typical outcomes of a Stage I analysis are a request for additional information from the property to clear up gray areas, or communication that a decision not to pursue the opportunity was reached. I should add that a thorough understanding of the Stage II analysis is required in order to make the necessary "quick" answers in a Stage I review—more on this below.

Here's a sampling of typical Stage I questions that would warrant a Yes/No response:

Brand Positioning
Is the sponsorship aligned with our brands' attributes?

Potential Distribution
Are there opportunities for retailer involvement?

Audience
Is the sponsorship aligned with current target consumers?

Customer Relations
Does the sponsorship provide opportunity to improve relationships with customers?

Geography
Does the property provide appropriate coverage?

Title Rights
Is there opportunity for "sole" (e.g. the title sponsor) ownership?

Corporate
Are there opportunities for integration with corporate properties and/or other divisions?

The challenge is keeping this Stage I tool kit as simple in scope as possible while addressing critical business and brand goals.

Stage II. The second stage analysis, comprising a detailed quantitative spreadsheet with numerically weighted goals and objectives, drives the in-depth analysis necessary to determine if an opportunity/property is well-aligned with business goals, brand attributes and other requirements. This set of detailed questions drills down into the elements of a successful sponsorship from the company's specific business-goals perspective. Each question is assigned a numerical answer, rather than a simple yes or no, and is further subject to a multiplier that allows the company to weight the relative importance of each aspect. Those elements considered critical to success get a higher multiplier and in the end contribute more to the overall score. In the tournament example above, it might be determined that it is very important to have the company's 20 top dealers present at the sponsored event as a component of landing new business. If this opportunity is lacking, the property's score will be very low. If the property offers an optimal environment for positive dealer involvement, it will score well.

Here's a sampling of a few Stage II questions:

Brand
Brand Alignment—5
Brand Importance—3
Identification with Brand Target Group—5

Distributor
Distributor Involvement—5
In-store Point of Sale—3
Cross Promotions—4
Event importance to Community—3

Audience
Consumer Identification—5
Importance—5
Reach/frequency—4

Customer Relations
Access Quality—5
Interaction ease/difficulty—5
Pre-Activities—2
Post-Activities—2

Outcomes from a Stage II analysis are likely to be a further conversation about the suitability of the opportunity as a prerequisite to begin talks or further negotiation and planning, or a communication indicating that the property failed to meet the secondary hurdles.

Importantly, the results of the Stage II analysis provide a very clear roadmap for negotiation. They also provide the basis for the eventual development of dashboards (referring to its visual comparison to a vehicle dashboard that provides information in a very concise format to the drive—speed, fuel, engine temperature, etc.)—our term for one-page reports on the health of a sponsorship relationship.

TAKE-AWAY

In pursuing an enlightened Six Sigma-based sponsorship management approach, a company may choose among establishing an in-house function and developing this expertise for itself, completely farming the job out or crafting a hybrid approach, where an agency with expertise in the field serves a role in the screening process. Maybe the initial improvement steps were taken with the assistance of a sponsorship success counselor, maybe not. The point is, the Six Sigma discipline requires that any breakthrough gains that have been made in the management of sponsorship must be maintained, if not advanced.

Most likely, a company will find that its Six Sigma-based approach to the business need of improving sponsorship management would be considered a strategic effort, prioritized at certain areas within business units or functional areas of the organization. Simple problem-solving—targeting a nagging and persistent dissatisfaction, perhaps even one that has been the focus of earlier but unsuccessful improvement efforts—is another on-ramp to Six Sigma.

Regardless of the form being entertained, the sponsorship managers of most companies probably will want to know early on what the cost of success will be. Of course, individual circumstances will determine the answer. But with almost US $30 billion (Source: IEG) being spent on sponsorship globally each year, enlightened sponsors are certain to have the cost of success question ranked equally with the need to proactively define success. And the difference between them may be a razor's edge.

6

Design for Six Sigma

Let's review where we are so far in the DMAIC process. We have thus far examined the philosophy behind Six Sigma and how it can be applied to sponsorship. We then took this one step further in establishing the importance of very specific business goals to complete the Define stage. The Y Discernment process and Stage I and II toolkits have constituted the bulk of our study so far—and rightly so because without this vital and important groundwork we could not continue to the MAIC (measure, analyze, improve and control) phase.

Now, armed to the teeth with solid, actionable business and brand objectives, we must assure that we can measure and analyze how successful we are in achieving those objectives, how to improve what we have achieved and to control the gains made in the process improvement.

This chapter will focus on taking the objectives and turning them into a set of sponsorship measurement parameters (or in the case of an initial engagement with a property, a set of negotiation parameters). We will produce a set of success objectives to ensure the investment in the property will yield a strong return. The following chapters will explain how we use the Design of Experiments (DOE) process to allow us to constantly improve our process and the yield against the objectives. Finally, we will explain how we track and analyze progress to ensure we are controlling our gains through dashboards. Let's start with how we design property relationships to meet goals.

DESIGN FOR SIX SIGMA (DFSS)

Like all Six Sigma processes, DFSS has its origins in the manufacturing realm. It is a process that starts with what the end customer wants and then designs the product/service/experience to meet those expectations. One interesting process designed to help with this phase is the Voice of the Consumer (VOC) method. It's begun by interviewing the consumer on what it is they think is important in the item under design and then building the item to meet those critical consumer expectations. By meeting these expectations, the product is much more likely to gain quick consumer trial, adoption and eventual advocacy.

Here's a brief example from the real world. Financial analysts recently faulted mobile phone manufacturer Nokia—one of the leaders in the field—for ignoring the VOC in its quest to build the next greatest cell phone. While Nokia focused on high-tech interactive functions such as multi-player game play, what consumers really wanted were affordable clamshell phones with embedded low-resolution digital cameras so they could share informal photos with their friends. Thus Nokia found itself with shrinking market share and an underperforming stock price, even though it may have had a temporary technology leadership. It was simply the wrong technology at the wrong time. This doesn't mean Nokia was wrong in the long run, but in the short run the company had to scramble to add new value priced products.

By using VOC up front, the company could have made engineering and product cycle decisions based on goals firmly rooted in business realities, such as what the consumer really wanted and thus producing sales. As a result, it likely would have maintained market share, better timed its new product introductions and still could have been first to market with next-generation features when the time was right.

What a revolution this represents for the world of sponsorship! Metaphorically, instead of taking the cell phone that is being offered and trying to live with it—which means we would still need to carry a digital camera or web-enabled PDA—we can tell the cell phone manufacturer that what we really need is one device that combines these features. So in applying this to a sponsorship in Rugby World Cup, for example, it may make far more sense to forgo large blocks of game tickets for the opportunity to do product sampling on the stadium grounds.

This is the basic theory that drives the Six Sigma sponsorship management design process. We (the principals) decide what WE need from a property in order to make the relationship fruitful. We DO NOT accept, *prima facie*, what the property offers as the only possible solution. Their offer is almost by definition what THEY need—not what WE want. This is quite a radical shift in thinking from traditional design methods.

Take-a-Note: In manufacturing, design of a new product can center on many varied objectives such as:

Least expensive solution—perhaps a plastic knob instead of a wood grain knob.
Highest volume solution—easily fabricated from raw stock, facilitating quick alterations to meet specifications.
Common part solution—often linked to least expensive and highest volume solutions (same chassis for a vehicle which may not be optimum for any particular vehicle design but will ultimately help to accelerate time to market, keep costs low, etc.).
Most reliable—perhaps safety or reliability is a key issue.
Lightest material—aircraft parts often sacrifice many design criteria for weight.
Etc.

The fundamental difference between designing to the objectives listed above and our DFSS process is our focus on building a relationship with a property—from the very start—that is meant to deliver on Six Sigma objectives. We seek to establish this more mutually beneficial partnership through the use of an illuminated and instructive process centered on goal achievement.

The theory in action. So let's examine how this entire new paradigm works in our sponsorship model. We already have defined business goals in the Y discernment process and the subsequent Stage I and II Toolkits.

Our application of Design for Six Sigma (DFSS) simply requires taking those objectives and turning them into actionable sponsorship activities.

Here's an example: Our goal is to increase product sales of a small-to-medium business by 10 percent in the Southeast United States over the next year. During the Y discernment process, we have identified three sub-goals (X's) that can be affected by sponsorship—they are:

1. Provide incentives to recruit new distributors

2. Demonstrate the value of our product vs. the competitor

3. Demonstrate the superior aspects of our product vs. the competitor

How will we know we are being successful in our achievement of the goals? We might set the following success parameters:

1. Entertain 100 high potential distributors during the year

2. Ensure 100 percent of all sponsorship venues have staffed booths that provide a personal explanation of the value of our product

3. Ensure 100 percent of all sponsorship venues have a personal demonstration of our product vs. the competitors

Now let us consider a property such as a NBA sponsorship opportunity. The opportunity is presented with the normal package of perks and benefits in exchange for $X. These include:

Media placement
Tickets
Suite passes
Parking
Event branding
Etc.

In a review of business objectives we realize that all the media placement and event branding in the world, without other supporting elements, will not help us deliver on the objectives outlined above.

We can now formulate a plan to address what WE NEED from the potential relationship—not what the property may want to offer. We can easily list out the following:

1. VIP ticket packages for 100 guests over the course of the season

2. Multiple product brochure distribution points throughout the stadium with guaranteed placement at key points

3. Two product demonstration booths measuring 10 feet by 20 feet located at the main entrances

This, we have "designed" the relationship with the property based on two key considerations:

1. The property must help achieve stated business goals and activities,

2. As important, we know EXACTLY what we will consider as a successful meeting of the goals!

Now there is no guesswork as to how goals will be met—we have defined achievable objectives that can be activated against, measured and improved.

TAKE-AWAY

To complete the DFSS phase, we simply repeat this exercise for each brand and business objective, turning them into actionable and measurable plans.

To be sure, this can be a challenging process. Often, a group new to this process will struggle, if not become stymied, by perceived impasses in defining how we can use sponsorship to reach certain brand and business objectives. This is quite normal. It takes enormous creativity and experience to produce a comprehensive plan that will translate to measurable results. Based on PRISM's collective experience in this aspect of sponsor-

ship, we suggest the following might be helpful in completing this critical
task:

1. Engage the properties from the start. Up to this point in the pro-
    cess the focus has been entirely centered on goal development, Y
    discernment process and Stage I and II Tool Kit develop-
    ment—none of which necessitates any involvement with the
    properties. That all changes here! Make sure the property under-
    stands what the goals are and how much their help is needed.
    Don't alienate the property by dropping a whole new set of suc-
    cess goals on them. Most good properties employ staff to make
    sure sponsors' goals are met. Most sponsors NEVER fully use that
    staff—except for more tickets, passes, parking passes, etc.—you
    get the picture.

2. Make sure the very top decision makers in the marketing/sales/PR
    area of the company are completely bought in to this new process.
    Ideally, they would have been involved from the very begin-
    ning—particularly during goal development and Y discernment.
    But assuming they were only peripherally involved at that point,
    engage them now. This may sound simple, but it rarely is. Proper-
    ties can complain to these decision-makers about the process and
    you will want the management on your side. Believe me, this is
    the easiest sell you will ever have to make to your management.
    Your essential selling message is: you'll help them justify (in case
    of an audit, for example) the current investments; create measure-
    ment criteria for success with all the properties (current and pro-
    spective); ensure a sound return on investment rationale; and turn
    the properties into partners who are actively engaged in truly help-
    ing meet brand and business goals.

3. Hopefully this point is moot by this stage, but if it hasn't occurred
    already, find a sponsorship consulting firm that understands this
    process and can help guide you through the entire transformation.
    Obviously, I recommend PRISM as the world's leading firm in
    this area. However, if you have an existing relationship with a

company, ask them if they can take on this type of paradigm-changing sponsorship management methodology.

4. Find a black belt within your company, or at your sponsorship agency, who can help guide the DFSS, DMAIC and DOE processes. Not just any black belt will do. They must believe in the application of Six Sigma in the marketing world and be prepared for a wild ride in its application. If you don't have a black belt available, or if your company has not yet adopted the Six Sigma infrastructure, ensure that your sponsorship agency has the requisite black and green belts to guide this process.

Following the above guidelines can help make the DFSS process to be smooth and efficient in its eventual rollout.

7

Improve Phase—Design of Experiments (DOEs)

A key advantage in using the Six Sigma methodology is the ability to analyze the data and make continual improvements. Design of Experiments (DOEs) is the true power tool of the Analyze and Improve phase of DMAIC (define, measure, analyze, improve, control).

We already have addressed how several different aspects of analysis can be used to illuminate the management of sponsorship in achieving brand and business objectives. The key concept to remember is that any analysis must be coherent to the end user. This means that an analysis of Internal Rate of Return, another common financial tool used to determine the relative merit of competing alternative investments, will make little sense to a company that considers Net Present Value its chief yardstick. In order for sponsorship to fit this company context, its performance must be presented in the analytical terms the company commonly uses. And I would advise against inventing too many new metrics as this will raise barriers to acceptance.

To do this, we must explore the central tool of continual improvement—Design of Experiments (DOEs). DOEs are extremely useful tools for analysis and improvement. They allow us to identify what variables in a process or event have the greatest impact on the results we are trying to achieve.

FUNDAMENTALS OF DOE

You were probably first introduced to a similar concept of experimentation in grammar school science. The basic premise is that certain elements of a process are held constant while other elements are varied. We experiment with different variables to affect the outcome. The desired outcome can be to maximize or minimize certain results. For instance, we may want to maximize the number of people attracted to a football game tailgate event. On the other hand, we also may want to minimize the amount we spend per person in attracting them to the same event. Rather a yin-yang example if you think about it.

The central question revolves around what to hold constant and what to vary. The complexity of multiple variable experiments makes it challenging to ensure that we know the changes made to the variable elements did in fact affect the outcome of the entire experiment.

Take-a-Note: In the 1920s a school of thought emerged that said if you vary only one variable in an experiment it will take too long to determine the maximum or minimum result. Thus, in manufacturing Six Sigma it is quite common to vary two to three variables at a time. Using now common statistical analysis, one can determine which of the two to three variables had the greatest affect on the outcome and realign the next experiment to emphasize that significant variable.

We already covered the impact on analysis of the complex and "noisy" sponsorship environment. This noise makes understanding the impact of many variables difficult to ascertain. Remember, this noise could prevent us from ascertaining the efficiency (or Z Score) of some investments.

It is for this reason that I believe that changing more than one variable in a sponsorship DOE is not advisable. This may be reconsidered with the help of a black belt if the particular sponsorship engagement lends itself to good analysis. Otherwise, make it a rule to stick to altering one variable per DOE.

Credit card name acquisition 101. So let's jump right into an example. A consumer credit company (read: credit cards) has been sponsoring a series of concerts. The objective we wish to analyze is the goal to acquire qualified names which the company can later call upon for the possible issuance of a credit card.

During the past few months the company has placed and staffed a tent outside the concert venues. The cost to run this event (tent rental, staff, other material costs) has averaged $1,000 per event. At each event they have acquired 1,000 names—making the acquisition cost per person $1. The main incentive for the consumer to complete the mini application is a branded T-shirt. Bear with me here on these fictitious numbers for the sake of illustration—I know the costs are often wildly different than the example here—I am using the figures for ease of calculation.

Due to other budget pressures, the company wants to minimize this cost of acquisition and wants to experiment with alternatives to lower the cost to run the events or raise the number of acquired names per event—both of which will result in a lower acquisition per name cost.

Let's assume we have already explored other ways to lower the costs—buying the tents, paying the staff less, etc. None of these potential reductions will make a significant impact on the overall cost of the program and thus the acquisition cost per name. So we must turn to the other possible way to lower the acquisition cost per name—increasing the number of names acquired per event.

Using the DOE technique, several options are brainstormed for consideration. After deliberation, two experiments are agreed upon:

1. Offering an incentive of a cab drive home after the concert, and

2. Automatic entrance into a drawing for a trip for two to an upcoming concert, complete with backstage passes—winner announced at the end of the concert.

The next few concerts are staffed with the same agency people, using the same tent and relative location at the concert. The only thing that is materially varied is the incentive offer of a cab ride and a chance at the backstage experience, leveraging the special access we are able to obtain as event sponsors. For the sake of this example, let's assume that the total cost remains the same for all three offers.

After several concerts we have the following data:

Experiment	# of Names Captured	Cost	Average Cost per name
T-Shirt	1000	$1,000	$1.00
Cab Ride	1111	$1,000	$.90
Backstage Pass	1250	$1,000	$.80

We can see that the chance for a backstage experience has significantly better yield in average cost per name captured over the cab ride offer. Intuitively, this makes sense because special access is a well-known attraction for people who consider themselves fans, whether it is of sport, music or movies. However, it is important to note that both experiments resulted in better results than the previous events.

From this data we can now realign our efforts and resources to focus on the backstage pass DOE variant. In fact, we may eliminate the T-shirt offer completely and consider redesigning the cab ride offer in some way. The best course would be to start brainstorming additional offers to seek to improve the average cost per name.

TAKE AWAY

This was a simplified but illustrative example. It's important to remember that the process does not stop here—and, in fact, it never stops. At future events additional DOEs can be run to further refine and maximize the return on many important brand and business goals. This is the core beauty of the Six Sigma methodology—continual improvement. One never arrives at the goal—but constant movement toward it occurs—with assurance that it can always be made better. DOEs are an extremely powerful tool that can change the way a company looks at return on investment (ROI) in sponsorship. Whatever the current ROI is, it can always be made better through continual experimentation in process yield.

8

Dashboards

Having explained how to design the sponsorship relationships to meet our brand and business objectives, we now turn to how to gather, analyze and track the data that will determine goal attainment.

I believe the more simple the presentation of critical success data the better. No executive I have met likes to see a stack of data plopped down on his or her desk without some sort of summary and analysis of what it all means—usable knowledge. While there are many ways of presenting summary data, I have found the concept of a dashboard to be the most useful.

Dashboards are an essential management reporting tool in many corporations. At GE, they were developed within the context of the "four-block." Within my first week at GE, I was told we needed to prepare the four-block for an upcoming presentation. A four-block refers to the landscape-oriented report format divided into four distinct quadrants—or blocks. I was told nearly everything in life could be put into a four-block—including one's marriage if necessary.

The advantages of the block format are immediately obvious. It consolidates important data sources onto one page. This is just the essential information needed for a manager to understand how their operation or project is running. There is never a single, rigid format. Most blocks used a graphic to express essential data: a pie chart, bar chart, table, etc. And every block needs a take-away box that highlights the essential meaning of the block. This best practice was adapted to the Six Sigma process.

The four-block has evolved into the dashboard, which follows most of the same principles outlined above. It consolidates several important data points onto one page—or dashboard—that allows a busy manager to quickly understand how a business or project is performing.

I have successfully used the dashboard concept in every job I have had since my time with GE. Dashboards are easily adapted to all Six Sigma projects—but they are particularly efficient and effective for reporting on sponsorships. With our focus on accountability and measurability, they are the face of our process—the painted picture that expresses how well we are doing at what we set out to do. Let's look at them a little more in depth.

Dashboards get their name from their organization and depiction which is similar to a dashboard in an automobile. Let's look at a typical auto dashboard:

Notice how it is organized to give the busy and completely preoccupied driver essential information. A tachometer, speedometer, fuel gauge and other indicators communicate critical performance information.

There is a tremendous amount of data that is collected elsewhere in the car that is transmitted to the dashboard for eventual display. For instance, the odometer is a function of the wheel size and its rotational speed. It would be fairly meaningless to the driver to know how fast the wheels are turning—what is important is what that wheel rotational velocity means in terms of ultimate vehicle speed; if for no other reason than to avoid getting a ticket!

Without belaboring the comparison, it is important to point out that the car dashboard gives the driver only the information he or she needs. That is exactly what we strive to achieve in sponsorship dashboards—only the data that indicates if the sponsorship is "successful" and in process control.

So let's take a look at what a typical dashboard looks like:

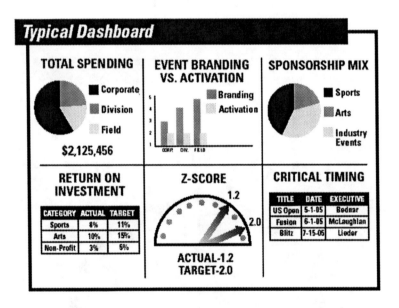

Dashboards are designed to reflect exactly what the company is most interested in knowing about its sponsorships. This will vary for nearly all companies. The dashboard can be composed of nearly any sort of management reporting needs important to the company. In the first introduction of a dashboard, companies often look to their sponsorship agency for guidance on what they should be tracking. So while there is no list of what companies should track, there are some common elements that many prove useful to all, at least initially.

Common elements of sponsorship dashboards include total spending, activation versus event branding, the sponsorship mix (or split, as we call it), return on investment, Z Scores (if possible), and the short-term event window. Let's take a look at each one.

Total spending. This may sound like a simple number to calculate—but it hardly ever is. There are many reasons why it is so difficult to compile, including:

1. Lack of centralized data—there is no simple way to "pull" the data from the system as events, entertainment, advertising, branding, hosting, promotion materials, etc., all exist in different account categories.

2. Lack of automated data—there is little automation available to easily compile the data. Often times, sponsorship hosting and other data are processed as expense statements and one-time invoices with sub-vendors which are not easily connected to sponsorship spending.

3. Varying and incongruent divisional reporting systems—in large organizations with sub-divisions and autonomous reporting companies, reporting systems, methodologies and formats often are different, making compilation difficult.

4. Lack of financial assistance—there are no assigned financial resources (people) to aide in finding the data.

5. Inability to identify spending—costs associated with sponsorship are hidden or dispersed among many differing accounts—regions, corporate, local, dealer associations, etc.

6. Conversion—typically firms involved in significant sponsorship deals "convert" a portion of their advertising and public relations budgets to support the sponsorship. For example, a $20-million

advertising budget might set aside 10 percent, or $2 million, for ads related to the company's involvement in Formula One, while one or more PR staff are assigned to attend races and provide media support.

In this day of computer networks and centralized administrative functions, point 3 above may seem incongruous. Yet my personal experience with Fortune 200 companies has shown this to be the case time and again—companies often don't standardize on some of the most basic functions, such as reporting systems. Why this is the case is unclear. It could be the rapid acquisition of companies through industry consolidation didn't allow for the complete integration of reporting systems. It may be due to the relative autonomy inherent in many successful global organizations—what will work in Rome will not work in Melbourne. It may be due to budget constraints—reporting systems integration is expensive. Regardless, do not assume that any reporting from differing organizations, particularly within the same corporation, will be easy to obtain and consolidate.

As you can see, discovering the TRUE costs involved in sponsorship can be quite difficult. The key is setting up a process of discovery that will consistently be applied across all reporting entities as you design your dashboard.

Activation vs. event branding. Activation usually is defined as doing something—integration with other communications channels, co-sponsor involvement, leveraging trade relationships, etc.—with your sponsorship other than paying rights fees that most often lean most heavily toward event branding.

As an example, a company may pay $100,000 to become the title sponsor of an event. This would be identified and counted as branding or rights fees. The rights fees may include tickets, parking, and even company or product branding on signage at the event. The activation element in this calculation would be what the company would then spend on interfacing with event attendees or fans with activities such as product displays, product sampling or contests, as well as the costs of participating in the event (flights, hotels, meals for company executives, journalists and VIP guests, etc.).

Sponsorship mix. We also call this "the split." Displayed as a pie chart, it shows the percentage mix of each major element in which the sponsoring company participates. This often includes sports, arts, entertainment, not-for-profit and industry events. It helps the company understand if their portfolio of sponsorship properties is in balance to expectations.

Return on investment. This is normally a table format, allowing the company to quickly understand its return on investment (ROI). ROI data can vary in reporting format depending on what is most important to the company. For instance, some companies may want to know what the ROI is by sponsorship mix (or segment); some may want to know by property, by geographic region, by division, etc. As in all dashboard elements, it is most useful when the company determines what it really needs to understand in order to make considered management decisions.

Z Scores. If the company has repetitive events—repetitive being an important distinction—that allow for the calculation of Z Scores, this is often displayed in a table format. Just like the ROI table, what is reported is completely dependent upon what the company finds most important to understand. Often it will mimic the ROI format—so if ROI is reported by division, the same is often true for Z Scores.

The short-term events window. Most companies want to know what is coming up in the next three months or so. This is the most widely varying table in most dashboards. Some companies only want to know what events are on the horizon, others want to know which company executives will be attending important sponsorships, when major spending decisions are due, etc. Again, the company knows what is most important to it and will easily adapt this part of the dashboard to their needs.

KEEP IT SIMPLE

So having reviewed some common elements in a sponsorship dashboard, we need to address the challenge of different levels of data compilation. Many corporations have several divisions or companies all spending resources in the sponsorship area making simple compilation challenging. This will be very company-specific. However, a simple design will help in organizing the data:

1. Design one common dashboard into which all divisions report. Again, simple, but we don't want differing reporting formats that then need to be manipulated or converted to the final summary report.

2. Each division should have a clear system to collect the data by specific dates.

3. There should be three basic levels of reports

    a. Division or company level. This may be extended further into the company division level if needed. For example, this could be compiled for each division by geographic area, or business segment, etc.

    b. Corporate level activities.

    c. Corporate roll-up or summary level report that takes into account the divisions or companies as well as the major corporate level activities.

The other major consideration in dashboard administration is the manner in which the data are reported.

TAKE-AWAY

Automation. Companies would prefer to have a completely automated process in order to minimize the amount of time their employees devote to data retrieval. Unfortunately, for the reasons described above, this is often a very difficult task. In addition to the infrastructure reasons cited above, there is the considerable cost involved with automating anything within a large company. In meetings around the globe, we have had several clients say they would like to have the information real time—meaning web-based or accessed via an intranet. This initial enthusiasm is quickly dashed when the costs involved with this kind of automation are presented.

Manual compilation. This is often the only practical solution, particularly when a company is first deploying the dashboard system. Here is a simple process to help ensure setting up a reliable reporting system.

1. Assign one person to update the dashboards. This compilation may be assigned to someone within the company or its sponsorship agency. This person is identified as the dashboard controller.

2. Assign one person at each company or division to report the data to the dashboard controller.

3. Unless the company has a tried and tested data sharing system that easily could be adapted for the sponsorship reporting needs, develop a simple Excel or other type of spreadsheet program to allow for easy reporting and integration of data.

4. Use an e-mail reminder system to prompt timely submission of data.

5. Use exception reporting to identify when data are not be submitted on time.

This should be a major job duty for the dashboard controller. In fact, most of our clients have our agency perform this function for them. After the system is established, the people harvesting data at the division or company should be able to compile and report this data with relative ease.

9

Summary

The important message of this Summary is that you need not be intimidated by the apparent complexity of Sponsorship Six Sigma. The first time we tried to ride a bike it seemed a daunting task. But once the basic skills were mastered, a whole new world of mobility opened up! Once you climb on Six Sigma, keep pedaling and remember that the key improvements to sponsorship management that this process provides are very real.

There is an existing context. First, significant gains are made with the adoption of the DMAIC process. This can be executed in an extremely aggressive manner with intense and in-depth application—OR, it can be executed as simplistically as starting with the commitment to Defining what is to be accomplished in sponsorship and then broadly applying the rest of the MAIC process. Successful application does not portend the complete roll-out to every individual company and every sponsorship. In fact, we recommend a judicious and measured application within an existing sponsorship framework.

We have many clients that have taken a crawl-walk-run attitude. This means start easy—with a few of the company's sponsorships or with one division, and generate a few success stories. This is the crawl phase. When considering expanding the application, or walking, often it is decided to apply this methodology to one full segment of the sponsorship business. This could be complete application through DOEs in one division or for one segment of sponsorship such as sports. The running phase begins when, through many small and intermediate successes, the management feels confident in rolling it out as a complete program for their company.

Second, you will enter upon a path of continual improvement—an unending "do-loop," in computer parlance. You will establish a new foundation or baseline of performance measurement—and as important—a new expectation for sponsorship property results. A simple perk package and/or signage will no longer be justification for large investment dollars.

Coping with Change. Recall in Chapter 1 the discussion of sponsorship today, in which I described how the management of sponsorship came to be in its present state of evolution: that odd mix of benefits and risks with much untapped potential. But we must remember that it is through a process of continuous change in the past—which will continue in the future—that things get to be the way they are. In other words, new forms of knowledge will continue to be advanced and new practices will be introduced.

If we recognize that integrating change with what exists is the order of the day, we must also acknowledge the associated inherent challenges. Comedian Bob Newhart had a great reply to his sit-com wife's accusation that he resisted, fought and hated change. "No, Emily, I just like things they way they are!" Whether we recognize it or not, change is always on the horizon and it can be a positive experience. The use of Six Sigma in an organization, whether it's applied to sponsorship or another area, can present challenges as well as opportunities.

Take-a-Note: As suggested by Pande & Holpe, here are a few tips and hints that will better prepare you to thrive in such a situation.

Learn all you can about why the initiative is being implemented. Understanding the goals and objectives will help you anticipate what you can do to make a contribution. Clearly defining what is adding value—thus qualifying as important—and what is not important is critical in achieving business goals of all kinds, not just sponsorship.

Expect some confusion. Implementing anything in today's organizations is never perfect. Plans will change, roles will evolve, key stakeholders get reassigned, and projects get launched and revamped or even abandoned. It's all part of organizational change and shouldn't discourage anyone from benefiting from the good aspects of change.

Think of your job as a part of a chain of activities that seeks to be well-organized and efficient. When changes occur, which can be difficult if you're comfortable with the ways things have always been done, remember, it's for a good reason.

Take advantage of learning opportunities and take responsibility for your own learning. In acquiring knowledge of any kind, it's best to plan on working hard but expecting to gain a lot.

All you have to fear is fear itself. Sometimes it's fear of change; sometimes fear of being blamed for the problems that are being analyzed. Look at things as a positive opportunity to make the situation better.

Prepare for the long haul. Six Sigma-based initiatives are not merely quality initiatives, they are business initiatives. Many other past improvement efforts have fallen by the wayside because improvements never became ingrained in the way people think and manage. Six Sigma is sure to evolve but it seems likely to be around for quite awhile.

There's no template for developing skills to use in the new decision-making model I propose for sponsorship. And improving processes—sponsorship and otherwise—should be a never-ending activity. Mostly, it's got to do with attitude. The main areas to work on are these:

Ability to see the big picture. We all seek to become experts in our own field or in multiple fields. But the ability to see and make decisions based on what works best for the end customer and the whole process is important. Recall the discussion of business objectives versus marketing objectives in Chapter 3.

Ability to gather data. For those who consider themselves "statistically challenged," don't worry. The skills needed for a successful Six Sigma approach to sponsorship are the ability to prioritize the recording of facts, explain them and separate them from guesswork, not be a statistical magician.

<u>Ability to question or break through your old assumptions</u>. At one time, everybody "knew" the Earth was flat. At one time, everybody "knew" the 4-minute mile was sacrosanct. At one time, everybody "knew" hard-sell ads were the thing. You get what I mean. Hanging on too tightly to conventional wisdom can stop change altogether.

<u>Ability to work collaboratively</u>. Sharing ideas, not just giving advice, leads to better ways of teaming up, and valuing opinions that lead to the development of solutions that benefit the greater good—usually starting with customers.

<u>Ability to thrive on change</u>. Unlike the Bob Newhart character who is in denial, change will happen whether we like it or not. Of course, change for no good reason can be bad. But change that helps get things done right is seldom condemned. The trick is to make change work for you.

<u>Begin your journey to enlightenment</u>

This book has laid out a new paradigm for sponsorship. That paradigm centers on measurement—*Sponsorship's Holy Grail*. No longer do you have to settle for the rationalization that sponsorship is an art form that can't be fully understood, or that a particular association is someone's pet project.

Our clients believed, at least in the hearts at some level, that the salesperson justifying the company's interest in sponsoring a golf tournament had true and real justification. "You simply cannot get a six hour meeting with the client under any other circumstances," is the oft-quoted refrain. They knew all along that was true.

Our clients knew in their hearts that it made complete sense for an automotive company to sponsor car racing. How could that possibly not be true? Win on Sunday, sell on Monday has been a race sponsorship truism for decades (quite similar to golf equipment sponsorship). They thought that it made sense—that it had to be true.

But without the data to back up those conclusions, how could they really be sure? Companies don't justify new plant and equipment expenses because they "know" they can find a product to produce in the facilities or have a "gut feeling" about production capacity. But those same executives willingly accept that sponsorship is some sort of mystical art or an immeasurable marketing and sales activity.

The methodology outlined in this book turns that philosophy on its head. Sponsorship not only can be measured, it can be held accountable to brand and business objectives just as any other function or process in a responsible company can.

You now owe it to your company, your shareholders and yourself to take the yoke of responsibility on your own shoulders and start this process now. Admittedly, the path to sponsorship enlightenment is a long haul. It is a journey that never reaches conclusion—but every stride produces continued improvement that finds its way right to the bottom line. There is no reason to delay or wait for the perfect opportunity—even the simplest or narrowest applications of this process will wildly change your ability to understand what exactly you are getting out of your investments.

You now have a map to the Holy Grail. All the mysteries have been unlocked. The route is clear. It's your fiduciary responsibility to follow it.

978-0-595-34812-1
0-595-34812-2

Printed in the United States
64601LVS00004B/541-543

9 780595 348121